HSOAC
HOMELAND SECURITY
OPERATIONAL ANALYSIS CENTER

THE EMERGENCY MANAGEMENT INSTITUTE AT 70

From Civil Defense to Emergency Management in an Education and Training Institution

PATRICK S. ROBERTS

PREPARED FOR THE EMERGENCY MANAGEMENT INSTITUTE AND THE FEDERAL EMERGENCY MANAGEMENT AGENCY

This research was published in 2023.
Approved for public release; distribution is unlimited.

About This Report

The Federal Emergency Management Agency's (FEMA's) Emergency Management Institute (EMI) celebrated its 70th anniversary in 2021. EMI plays multiple roles as an education and training provider, thought leader, and site for the development of emergency management (EM) doctrine. The disaster threats and hazards at the top of the national agenda have changed, and EMI aims to provide training content that reflects the dynamic threats and hazards confronting emergency managers today. EMI faces the challenge of determining how best to carry out its unique mission in the EM ecosystem while remaining agile enough to continue to meet the needs of emergency managers of the future. The institute and its predecessor, the Civil Defense Staff College (CDSC), faced similar challenges in finding its place in an education and training ecosystem, and a consideration of how EMI overcame these challenges in the past can inform strategy and planning today. EMI evolved in tandem with the field of EM. This report categorizes the field's development into three eras—civil defense (CD), EM, and homeland security—and documents my conclusion that, as of 2020, the field could be entering a new era of all-hazards management. Therefore, EMI will need to adapt by building new partnerships and providing core disaster management skills applicable to a wide variety of events. EMI also has an opportunity to grow from a technically focused institution into a thought leader and educator of the next generation of EM leaders.

The larger project of which this report is a part is intended to provide support to EMI's strategy development and implementation, including the EMI Anywhere effort to make training available to emergency managers wherever they are, at any time in their careers, through multiple modes and locations.[1] The project also contributes to the FEMA 2022–2026 strategic plan's effort to "modernize [EMI's] operational design" and to make EMI the "nation's emergency management college."[2] Transforming EMI into an EM "college" is, in some sense, a return to its roots as CDSC. CDSC did not issue degrees, but it was a center of learning for members of the field. A companion report, *The Emergency Management Institute at 70: Options for the Future*, will pick up where this history report leaves off and analyze EMI's strategic positioning.

Although this history report is directly applicable to EMI, it might be of interest to other parts of FEMA and to other DHS components, as well as other agencies in the federal government and state, local, tribal, and territorial entities. Other education and training providers, including colleges and universities, might also be interested in how EMI both shaped and was shaped by the evolving professions of CD and EM and transformed its model of education. In addition, private-sector education and training, as well as EM, entities might be interested in the roles EMI might play in future training and education endeavors as the threats at the top of the national agenda evolve and new technologies make it easier for EMI to reach private-sector partners across the United States. Finally, this report might appeal to any audience interested in the history of CD, EM, and homeland security.

This research was sponsored by EMI and conducted within the Infrastructure, Immigration, and Security Operations Program of the Homeland Security Operational Analysis Center (HSOAC) federally funded research and development center (FFRDC).

---

1 In 2021, EMI adopted the EMI Anywhere strategy to train and educate emergency managers in the United States in any geographic location and at any time in their careers. See Jeffrey Stern, "EMI Anywhere," briefing slides, FEMA, U.S. Department of Homeland Security (DHS), July 2, 2021.

2 FEMA, *2022–2026 FEMA Strategic Plan: Building the FEMA Our Nation Needs and Deserves*, circa December 16, 2021d, p. 21.

About the Homeland Security Operational Analysis Center

The Homeland Security Act of 2002 (Public Law 107-296, Section 305, as codified at 6 U.S.C. § 185) authorizes the Secretary of Homeland Security, acting through the Under Secretary for Science and Technology, to establish one or more FFRDCs to provide independent analysis of homeland security issues. The RAND Corporation operates HSOAC as an FFRDC for DHS under contract HSHQDC-16-D-00007.

The HSOAC FFRDC provides the government with independent and objective analyses and advice in core areas important to the department in support of policy development, decisionmaking, alternative approaches, and new ideas on issues of significance. The HSOAC FFRDC also works with and supports other federal, state, local, tribal, territorial, and public- and private-sector organizations that make up the homeland security enterprise. The HSOAC FFRDC's research is undertaken by mutual consent with DHS and is organized as a set of discrete tasks. This report presents the results of research and analysis conducted under task order 70FA2021F00000027, The Emergency Management Institute (EMI) at 70 Years: Options for the Future.

The results presented in this report do not necessarily reflect official DHS opinion or policy.

For more information on HSOAC, see www.rand.org/hsoac. For more information on this publication, see www.rand.org/t/RRA1523-2.

Acknowledgments

I would like to thank many colleagues for their efforts and assistance. I am grateful to external reviewers Eric K. Stern and William L. Waugh for their comments on draft documents. At RAND, I thank Andrew Lauland for project management and editing assistance; Jason Thomas Barnosky, Shelly Culbertson, Aaron Clark-Ginsberg, and Edward Geist for editorial review; David M. Adamson and Matthew Sargent for editing assistance; Kevin J. Connolly, Shreya S. Huilgol, Daniel Kim, Samantha Ryan, and Eileen Young for research assistance; Yvonne K. Crane and Kristen Meadows for graphic design; Diane Egelhoff, Emily Haglund, and Olatunda Martin for document preparation assistance; Henry H. Willis for the management of HSOAC and the Infrastructure, Immigration, and Security Operations Program; and Terrence Kelly and K. Jack Riley for HSOAC leadership. At EMI, I thank Jeffrey D. Stern, Michael Sharon, Scott Kelberg, Jennifer Ogle, Scott Van Dermark, and other leadership and staff personnel for their guidance and support.

Although I am thankful for the assistance provided by those listed above and others, any errors or omissions should be attributed solely to me.

Summary

This report provides a seven-decade history of the Emergency Management Institute (EMI) and its predecessor organization, the Civil Defense Staff College (CDSC), from the founding of CDSC in 1951 to EMI in 2022. The report's purpose is to tell the story of these institutions' development within a broader context and to inform current strategy about EMI's future. EMI trains primarily state, local, tribal, and territorial (SLTT) officials in emergency management (EM). It also trains some federal officials and leaders in the nonprofit and private sectors and provides course materials for higher education.

The fiscal year (FY) 2022–2026 FEMA strategic plan calls for EMI to modernize its operational design and "to become the nation's emergency management college."[1] As a result, EMI is reconsidering its internal structure; its relationship to other parts of FEMA, DHS overall, and the rest of the federal government; and its relationship to the profession more broadly.

Emergency managers have been asked to respond to a growing number of hazards and disasters, including nontraditional missions, such as managing pandemic response and addressing homelessness. EMI will need to adapt to the increasing responsibilities of EM by building new partnerships and training professionals in disaster management skills applicable to a wide variety of events. EMI also has an opportunity to grow from a technically focused institution into a thought leader and educator of the next generation of EM leaders.

The Emergency Management Institute Evolved as Threats, Hazards, and the Concept of What Counts as a Disaster Changed

Throughout EMI's history, the hazards and threats at the top of the EM agenda have changed, and the field has evolved accordingly. The threat of missile attacks and nuclear war led to the creation of CDSC. Over time, fears of nuclear war faded, and concern about natural hazards and disasters increased, as did concern about social equity and the ways in which hazards and disasters can have disproportionate effects on marginalized populations. At the same time, some hazards and disasters (e.g., floods) remained constant and pervasive.

EMI both shaped and was shaped by the larger EM field. At key moments, EMI served as a source of expert advice and as a convener for members of the field. Throughout EMI's history, its training and education programs have communicated federal and national-level priorities to SLTTs. In some cases, EMI helped to communicate SLTT priorities to the federal government, as in the case of reforms to the EM system following Hurricane Katrina in 2005.

The Emergency Management Institute Evolved Its Organization, Curriculum, and Delivery Modes in Four Periods in Emergency Management

I identified four distinct phases in EMI's history based on important moments in that history and particular eras or, in scholarly terms, *institutional logics*. Institutional logics are not logics in the sense of a mathematical proof. Rather, they provide categories to describe a larger rhetorical and institutional environment. The

1 Federal Emergency Management Agency (FEMA), U.S. Department of Homeland Security (DHS), *2022–2026 FEMA Strategic Plan: Building the FEMA Our Nation Needs and Deserves*, circa December 16, 2021d, p. 21.

chapters in the report are organized according to these logics. The logics are defined by different sets of threats and hazards at the top of the agenda, rhetoric, and organizational approaches. As shown in Table S.1, the logics and their eras are

- civil defense (CD), 1951 to 1979
- EM, 1979 to 2001
- homeland security, 2001 to 2020
- expanded all-hazards, 2020 to the present.

The report's final chapter describes the fourth, which is an expanded all-hazards logic with more responsibilities for emergency managers. This period began in 2020 with the designation of FEMA as the lead agency for pandemic response. Although the all-hazards concept had always been part of FEMA doctrine, after 2020, EM more fully embraced all-hazards, including nonstandard missions outside of natural hazards (e.g., floods, fires, and hurricanes).

The logics are associated with events in EMI's organizational history, major disasters, and other developments in U.S. government and society. Figure S.1 shows some of the events discussed in the report.

The Emergency Management Institute's Focus Shifted from Civil Defense to Emergency Management

CDSC was created in 1951 at the dawn of the Cold War as part of the U.S. Department of Defense, and its defining logic was paramilitary. It trained CD leaders primarily from state and local governments to respond to external threats, both conventional and nuclear. The instructors were retired military officers who taught how to keep a city or community running in the wake of an attack.

In the 1960s, CDSC's curriculum broadened to include new training for radiological, chemical, and biological attacks. However, the waning focus on CD and the growing concern about the toll caused by natural hazards in the latter half of CDSC's history led the college to incorporate more programs related to natural

TABLE S.1
Comparing Institutional Logics

Institutional Logic	Years	Core Threats and Hazards	Form of Organization
CD	1951–1979	War, nuclear attack	Federal agencies, small state and local offices, volunteers
EM	1979–2001	Fire, flood, hurricane, earthquake, tsunami, radiological or industrial hazard	Small federal agency; grant to a state, locality, or survivor; state or local agency; core emerging profession; NIMS doctrine
Homeland security	2001–2020	Deliberate attack (most salient); terrorism, cyberattack, missile attack; natural or technological hazard; migration	Large federal agency, state or big-city agency, grant to a state or locality, disparate communities within homeland security; composed of multiple fields and professions
Expanded all-hazards	2020–	Natural or technological hazard, deliberate attack, pandemic, cyberattack, climate change, a social problem that impedes societal functioning (e.g., acute periods of homelessness)	Emergency managers as leading across boundaries using informal authorities and incident management skills; emergency managers as trusted brokers

NOTE: NIMS = National Incident Management System.

FIGURE S.1

Timeline of Events in Emergency Management Institute History

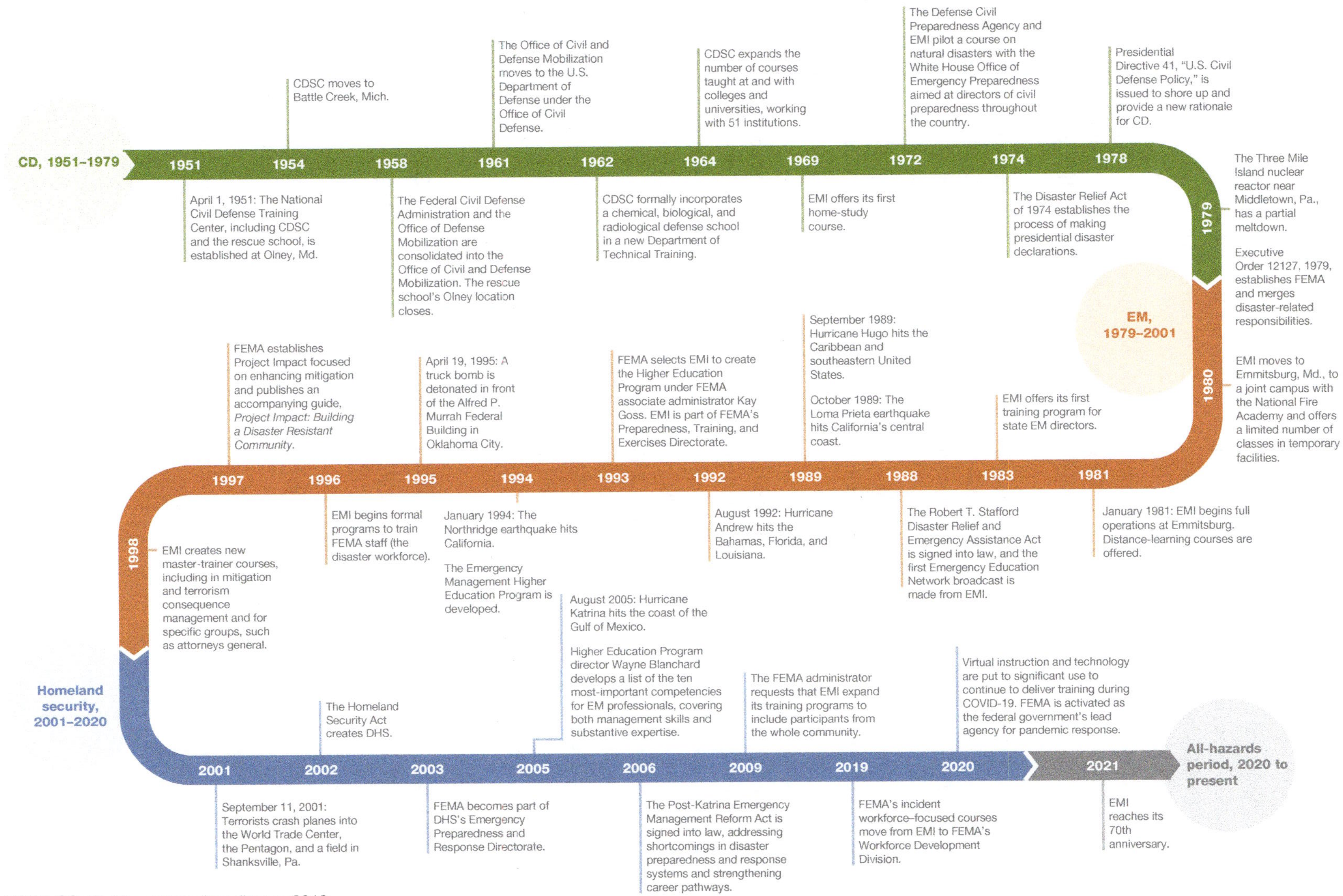

NOTE: COVID-19 = coronavirus disease 2019.

hazards and disasters over time. The roots of the United States' decentralized approach to EM training lie in the history of CD.

A series of hurricanes, floods, tornadoes, and earthquakes in the 1970s drew attention to the devastation caused by natural hazards. In the late 1970s, after pressure from state and local leaders, policymakers saw the need for a single federal entity to coordinate EM response and disaster relief. In 1979, FEMA was created to play this role. Accordingly, the education and training demands placed on EMI shifted from CD to disaster preparedness. CDSC was renamed *EMI* and it moved from Battle Creek, Michigan, to Emmitsburg, Maryland. At the same time, EM began to develop as a field.

EMI staff worked to bridge the gap between the CD and EM cultures. A 1983 FEMA report portrayed EMI's mission in its early years as "dialogue and role definition" among the various groups that make up EM: police, fire, emergency services, and public interest groups, among others. These dialogues stressed response to disasters more than mitigation or recovery.

Most instructors were hired through individual contracts, rather than being permanent staff. The instructor pool was drawn largely from state officials who were experts in a course's subject matter, state or local leaders of emergency exercises, college and university professors, or experts from federal labs. The use of instructors hired through individual contracts continued throughout EMI's history.

EMI adopted the all-hazards approach to EM—a framework that focuses on the capabilities needed to prepare for and respond to the full spectrum of emergencies and disasters. These capabilities include mitigation programs—programs to reduce the losses caused by disasters before they occur. During the 1990s, FEMA and EMI emphasized mitigation as a part of disaster preparedness.

Following the September 11, 2001, terrorist attacks and the creation of DHS in the early 2000s, EMI added a focus on homeland security, which included preparedness for and responses to the threats of terrorism and mass-casualty events. EMI offered new courses on homeland security issues but did not substantially shift away from EM following the creation of DHS. The creation of DHS brought new federal agency partners and processes, as well as new organizational layers, to EMI's work.

One innovation during the 2000s was programs to train officials in NIMS, following Homeland Security Presidential Directive 5's (2003) instruction to develop a single national approach to incident management. EMI did not develop NIMS, but it trained SLTT officials and nonprofit and private-sector leaders in a standardized approach to managing disasters and other incidents.

The Emergency Management Institute Remained Focused on Emergency Management Training as Other Institutions Pursued Related Fields

Over time, other educational institutions emerged offering education and training in homeland security and in chemical, biological, nuclear, and radiological preparedness. Since its rebranding as EMI in 1981 and move from Battle Creek, Michigan, to Emmitsburg, Maryland, EMI remained focused on EM at its core. EMI adapted its offerings as technology changed. It was an early adopter of instruction through videocassette and satellite broadcast, even as it brought students from across the country to its campus for in-person ("resident") courses. Figure S.2 shows one of the buildings at the in-person campus.

Demand among colleges and universities for courses in CD was never very strong, although CDSC built university partnerships. However, since its move to Emmitsburg, Maryland, and rebranding as EMI in 1981, EMI has provided course materials for use by colleges and universities. EMI's Higher Education Program built a network of EM degree programs in colleges and universities, and the number of programs grew from fewer than five in 1992 to roughly 150 in 2007 and more than 300 by 2018. Although colleges and universities provided degrees and professional associations offered certifications (such as the International Association

FIGURE S.2
Building N at the National Emergency Training Center Campus in Emmitsburg, Maryland

SOURCE: Reproduces a photograph from EMI, *Emergency Management Institute FY 2019 Annual Report*, draft, 2020.
NOTE: Building N was designed by the English-born architect E. G. Lind (1829–1909) in the Second Empire style. It was built in 1870 and renovated in 1987 and 1992. The building houses EMI and U.S. Fire Administration (USFA) staff.

of Emergency Managers' Certified Emergency Manager program), EMI remained focused on disseminating knowledge about EM and training SLTT officials. College students encountered EMI materials in college courses, and some took EMI courses, but EMI never offered degrees. EMI did not compete directly with colleges and universities, but it worked with them and the professional associations to build an emerging profession.

The Emergency Management Institute Trains More Than 800,000 Students per Year

EMI reaches a large number of students through a diversity of program types, locations, and lengths, including weeks on campus in Emmitsburg, Maryland; on-site trainings around the country; and independent study courses that can be completed at a student's own pace. As of FY 2022, the institute offered 86 resident course offerings, training 2,379 students at its campus in Emmitsburg. EMI's nonresident programs served 828,848 students in FY 2022, for a total of 2,110,403 course completions (some students took multiple courses). The total represents 20,667 instructor-led course completions and 2,110,403 completions through self-paced distance-learning training via the EMI Independent Study program.[2]

EMI courses are typically organized around four phases of EM: mitigation, preparedness, response, and recovery.[3] The courses cover natural hazards (e.g., earthquakes, floods, hurricanes), technological hazards (e.g., hazardous material, radiological accidents, chemical accidents), and terrorism. EMI also offers professional development, leadership, instructional design, public information, integrated EM, and train-the-trainer programs.

The Emergency Management Institute Has Helped the Emergency Management Profession Grow and Mature

Hurricane Katrina in 2005 drew attention to the threat of natural hazards. Many observers thought that the response to the storm proved that federal homeland security policy and organization had shifted too far in the direction of terrorism preparedness and away from preparing for and responding to large-scale natural disasters that overwhelmed states and localities. In response, the federal government strengthened the EM profession and career pathways. Again, EMI supported training in these career pathways for managers around the country. During this time, the field of EM grew in scope and complexity. In response, EMI developed an innovative course that integrated all EM into a single approach to preparing for and responding to crises. The four-day, exercise-based integrated EM course has become a cornerstone of EMI's curriculum.

The growing complexity and scope of EM could be due, in part, to the success of EMI and other institutions in building knowledge and competencies in the field, which resulted in emergency managers being given greater responsibilities.

EMI also contributed to diversifying a field that was traditionally white, male, and from military and public safety backgrounds. EMI's on-site programs offered opportunities for building networks and forming mentoring relationships. They also offered formal training and the opportunity to build credentials to allow new entrants into the profession. Diversity includes ability and disability, as well as race, ethnicity, and gender. Despite progress, the field remains less diverse in race, ethnicity, and gender than the general population. However, new nonprofit organizations, including the William Averette Anderson Fund, are building pipelines into the field and offer potential for collaboration with EMI.

Institutional Logics from Prior Eras Can Be Recombined

Despite changes in EMI and the field of EM as a whole and the variety of disasters and focusing events that took place, none of the various institutional logics that have shaped EMI ever wholly disappeared. This finding has three implications for EMI's future:

- Some old logics can be recovered. Policy, doctrine, and authorities (e.g., the Defense Production Act) for mobilization from the CD era can help deal with pandemics or national-scale events.
- Current leaders have a variety of strategic options to borrow from each of these areas or to recombine them.

[2] Senior EMI staff member, email to the author, October 6, 2022.

[3] EMI, "Emergency Management Institute Mission," webpage, last modified December 1, 2014.

- The existence of these multiple logics (missions, purposes, doctrines, practices, and terms) creates greater complexity and potential confusion. EMI will need to reconcile them to serve EM goals.

The Emergency Management Institute Is at a Crossroads and Has Options to Shape Its Future, Including Expanding Education Programs, Partnerships, and Thought Leadership

EMI is where expertise in the field is created and reinforced (in addition to some college and university programs and professional associations). EMI has focused the field on national-level disaster preparedness goals (e.g., the National Preparedness Goal) because it is housed in government. This stands in contrast to other fields, such as cybersecurity or business, in which expertise is more often developed in the private sector and colleges and universities than in government.

As EM enters a new era, EMI and the broader field are at a crossroads, as shown in Figure S.3. They could focus on a narrow variety of natural hazards, or they could broaden their reach to encompass a wider variety of threats and hazards. Yet another option would be to focus training and education on EM tools for planning, coordination, and incident command that could be used to address an expanding list of potentially uncertain threats and hazards. The history of EMI shows that the institute is likely to be asked to train and educate for new kinds of events.

If the field is to address new kinds of events and more-complex threats and hazards, it will need to expand its knowledge base through education that can address uncertainty, not just training for what is known in advance. Growing EMI's education activities in addition to more narrowly targeting training programs would build on its history. One area of continuity across the changes in EMI is the organization's function as a convener of experts and thought leaders through which it has contributed to theoretical and practical advancements in the fields of CD, EM, and homeland security.

Emergency managers have been given increasing responsibilities for a variety of nontraditional missions. FEMA's being given responsibility for leading pandemic response in 2020 might have signaled the beginning of an expanded all-hazards era. EMI has taken advantage of new learning technologies and partnerships with external institutions (e.g., colleges and universities and professional associations) throughout its history. As emergency managers are asked to lead responses to new kinds of events, EMI can support the profession by incorporating new learning technologies and building new partnerships. EMI has been an important linkage among emergency managers who are not connected in a hierarchical fashion but must work together to help people before, during, and after disasters.

FIGURE S.3
Three Options for the Emergency Management Institute

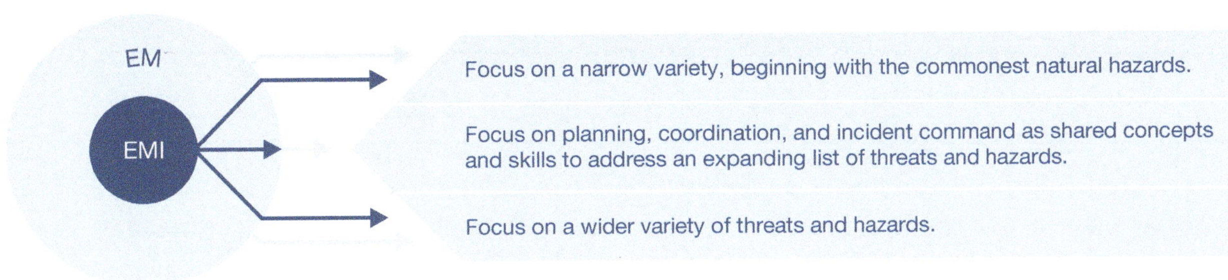

Research Approach

The overall approach to the research used the lens of *institutional logic*, which is a term used to analyze shared assumptions and practices. The central research questions were as follows:

- How did EMI evolve along with the professions it served?
- How did CDSC become EMI?
- What eras characterize the history of these organizations?
- What legacy does CD offer EM?
- What were the pivotal events and most-important programs in EMI's history?
- What insights does the history of EMI provide for the institution today and for the EM field?

To answer these questions, I conducted

- document analysis
- interviews and discussions.

The document analysis included government documents, research reports, peer-reviewed literature, and current and historical EMI materials. The primary data sources were documents, but interviews and discussions with the EMI sponsor team and five current or former senior EMI staff members with long tenures added context.

Contents

Figures and Tables

Figures

Tables

CHAPTER 1

Introduction

This report provides a history of the Emergency Management Institute (EMI) and its predecessor organization, the Civil Defense Staff College (CDSC), from the founding of CDSC in 1951 to EMI in 2022. The purposes of the history are to tell the story of these institutions' development and of the evolution of the emergency management (EM) field and to inform current strategy about EMI's future.[1] It is often said that people who fail to learn from history are doomed to repeat it.[2] History can also generate contextual insights that provide guidance for the present.

The Emergency Management Institute's Roles Have Evolved

EMI evolved from an initial focus on civil defense (CD) to address a broader menu of threats, including nuclear war, natural hazards, terrorist attacks, and pandemics. Throughout this transformation, EMI produced new courses, new modes of delivery, new partnerships, and new ideas to build the evolving profession of EM.

In addition, EMI played a role in shaping EM doctrine, although this role was often "invisible," according to one senior EMI official, who observed that, in addition to its educational function, the institution has often worked behind the scenes as a convener, assembling people from multiple levels of government, the nonprofit sector, colleges and universities, and private companies to meet to discuss and debate where the field stands and where it should go.[3] In doing so, it has shared concepts and practices that linked state, local, tribal, and territorial (SLTT) governments; nonprofits; and the private sector. Educating people from across this dispersed system has supported coordination among CD and EM entities, despite a lack of formal hierarchy. Thus, shared knowledge and professionalization through formal training and standardized processes contributed to building the EM profession.

EMI's delivery of education and training also evolved as postsecondary education changed. The share of Americans completing college grew steadily; more certifications emerged across all fields; educational achievement became more racially, ethnically, and gender-inclusive; and, in the 21st century, online learning became more common. EMI's practices have evolved alongside these trends. The institution has served practitioners in the emerging fields of CD and EM and contributed to shaping these fields.

EMI's programs provide both education and training. Education, as commonly defined by scholars, involves teaching higher-order critical thinking and conceptual skills without a particular applied purpose, while training aims at sharing knowledge about routines and standardized implementation of good practices

1 For convenience, I refer to the organization as *EMI* throughout, except when specifically referring to CDSC.

2 George Santayana, *The Life of Reason: Introduction and Reason in Common Sense*, Charles Scribner's Sons, 1905, p. 284.

3 Senior EMI staff member, interview 1 with the author, December 9, 2021.

to apply in application.[4] According to this distinction, EMI has offered both education and training, but, measured by the number of courses, it has offered more training than education.

The Emergency Management Institute by the Numbers

EMI has had a broad reach throughout its history. Totaling enrollments in 71 years of annual reports shows that EMI has trained 287,152 people in its resident (on-campus) courses. The true number is likely closer to 300,000 because of missing data and missing reports for some years. Adding nonresident (off-campus) courses puts the total in the millions. Nonresident courses include on-site instruction in government offices and universities around the country and self-study courses via mail correspondence, videocassette, and the internet.

EMI data over time show a growing number of courses and on-campus students despite erratic funding. The sharp drop in 2019, when courses moved online because of the pandemic, is an exception. The data in this report are divided into four eras in EMI's history, which represent approaches to EM. Data on the numbers of courses, on-campus students, and budgets are incomplete because of a lack of available data, but they do give a picture of trends over time. It is most useful to focus on high-level trends, given data limitations, and understand specific periods of time in more detail through the historical narrative in the report.

Data Sources

Data for EMI enrollment and numbers of courses come from annual reports from 1951 through 1985. Specifically, I used data from the education and training section of the annual reports of the parent organizations that housed CDSC and EMI.[5] However, I was not able to find annual reports or available enrollment and budget data for 1986 through 2007. For this period, I relied on EMI course catalogs for total resident (on-campus) courses per year. Budget data came from annual reports, except for the period of 2012 to 2021, for which I used data from U.S. Department of Homeland Security (DHS) congressional budget justification documents. (Data were consistently available in EMI annual reports only from 2008 to 2012.) Further limitations are described in the appendix.

Budgets, Enrollment, and Courses

Early budgets were modest, but CDSC experienced a significant budget increase in the early 1960s, with a peak in 1964, followed by decline (see Figure 1.1). Numbers of courses and graduates reached a peak in 1961. Cold War tensions were high during the early 1960s. During the 1961 Berlin crisis, the Union of Soviet Socialist Republics (USSR) demanded withdrawal of Western forces from Berlin, and the result was a partition of Berlin and the construction of the Berlin Wall. CDSC's parent organization, OCDM, expanded training and education efforts beyond CDSC residential courses beginning in 1960.[6] These new programs included the Civil Defense Adult Education Program, which trained more than 23,000 teachers. Other programs included in the budget totals in the 1960s but not strictly CDSC functions include medical self-help training, radio-

[4] Louis Menand, *The Marketplace of Ideas: Reform and Resistance in the American University*, W. W. Norton and Company, 2010, pp. 53–65.

[5] These organizations are the Federal Civil Defense Administration (FCDA) from 1951 to 1958, the Office of Civil and Defense Mobilization (OCDM) from 1958 to 1961, the Office of Civil Defense (OCD) from 1961 to 1972, the Defense Civil Preparedness Agency (DCPA) from 1972 to 1979, and the Federal Emergency Management Agency (FEMA) from 1979 onward.

[6] OCDM, *Annual Report of the Office of Civil and Defense Mobilization for Fiscal Year* [FY] *1959*, 1960, pp. 47–53.

FIGURE 1.1

Fiscal Year Funding for the Emergency Management Institute, 1951–2021

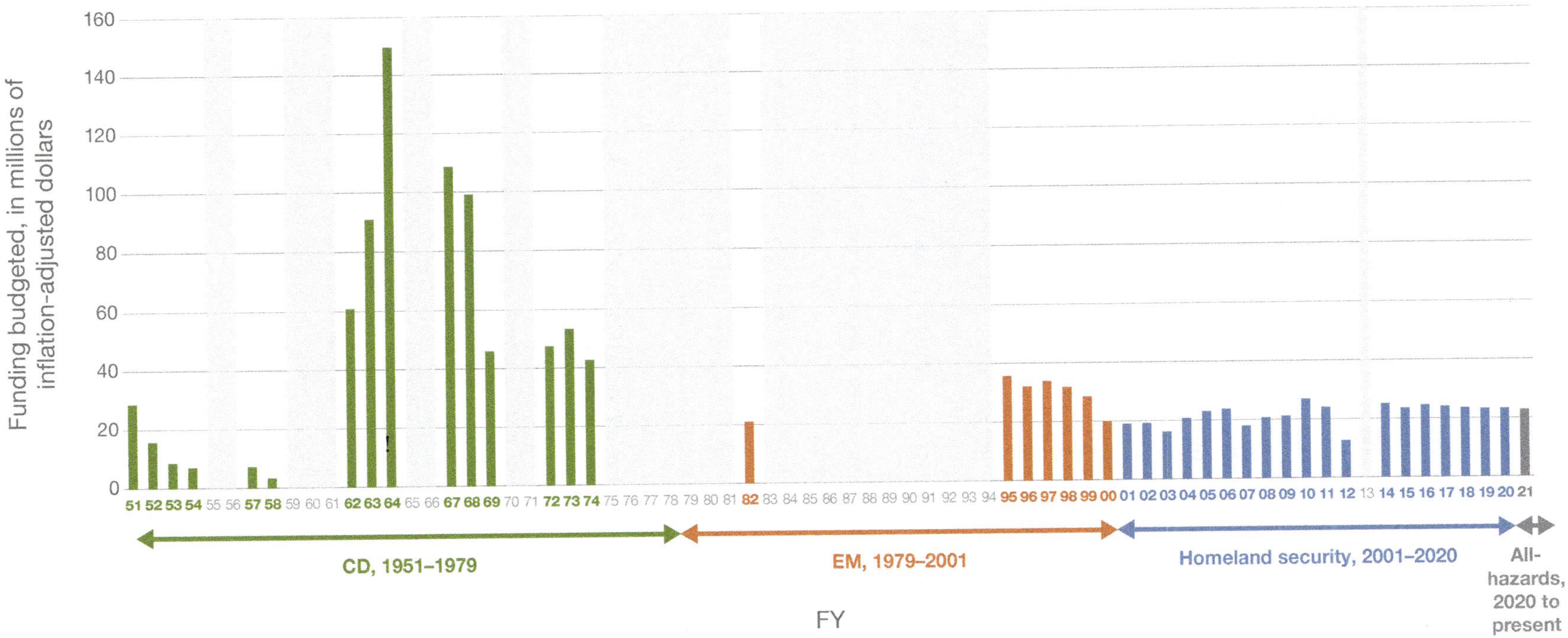

SOURCES: Features data from DCPA, *Civil Preparedness: A New Dual Mission—Annual Report Fiscal Year 1972*, December 15, 1972; DCPA, *Foresight: Annual Report FY 1973*, February 8, 1974; DCPA, *Taking Measure: Annual Report 1975*, June 30, 1975; DHS, *U.S. Department of Homeland Security Annual Performance Report: Fiscal Years 2012–2014*, April 1, 2013; DHS, fiscal year 2015 budget justification, c. 2015a; DHS, *Congressional Budget Justification: FY 2016*, c. 2016; DHS, *Congressional Budget Justification: FY 2017—Volume III, U.S. Secret Service, National Protection and Programs Directorate, Federal Emergency Management Agency, U.S. Citizenship and Immigration Services*, c. 2017; EMI, *FY 2008 Annual Report*, 2008; EMI, *FY 2009 EMI Annual Report*, 2009; EMI, *Fiscal Year 2010 Annual Report*, December 28, 2011; EMI, *Fiscal Year 2011 Annual Report*, May 29, 2012b; EMI, *Fiscal Year 2012 Annual Report*, May 1, 2013; EMI, *FY 2015 Annual Report*, 2015; EMI, *Annual Report Fiscal Year 2017*, 2017; EMI, *Fiscal Year 2018 Annual Report*, 2018; EMI, *Annual Report Draft*, 2019a; EMI, *Emergency Management Institute FY 2019 Annual Report*, draft, 2020; FCDA, *Annual Report for 1951 of the Federal Civil Defense Administration to the President and the Congress of the United States of America*, April 18, 1952; FCDA, *Annual Report for 1952*, 1953; FCDA, *Annual Report for 1953*, 1954; FCDA, *Annual Report for 1954*, 1955; FCDA, *Annual Report for 1955*, 1956; FCDA, *Annual Report for Fiscal Year 1956*, 1957; FCDA, *Annual Report for Fiscal Year 1957*, 1958; FEMA, *Budget Overview: Fiscal Year 2018 Congressional Justification*, c. 2017; FEMA, *Budget Overview: Fiscal Year 2019 Congressional Justification*, c. 2018a; FEMA, *Budget Overview: Fiscal Year 2020 Congressional Justification*, c. 2019a; FEMA, *Budget Overview: Fiscal Year 2021 Congressional Justification*, c. 2020a; FEMA, *Budget Overview: Fiscal Year 2022 Congressional Justification*, c. 2021a; OCD, *Annual Report of the Office of Civil Defense for Fiscal Year 1962*, 1962; OCD, *Annual Report of the Office of Civil Defense for Fiscal Year 1963*, 1963; OCD, *Annual Report of the Office of Civil Defense for Fiscal Year 1964*, December 28, 1964; OCD, *Annual Report of the Office of Civil Defense for Fiscal Year 1966*, 1966; OCD, *Annual Report of the Office of Civil Defense for Fiscal Year 1967*, 1967; OCD, *Annual Report of the Office of Civil Defense for Fiscal Year 1968*, 1968; OCD, *Annual Report of the Office of Civil Defense for Fiscal Year 1969*, December 20, 1969; OCDM, *Annual Report of the Office of Civil and Defense Mobilization for Fiscal Year 1958*, 1959; and OCDM, 1960.

NOTE: Gray indicates that I had no data for that year. Budgets are inflation-adjusted to 2021 dollars. I found no data for 2013. The budget justification was in the 2012–2014 report (DHS, 2013).

logical training, and rural CD training. The annual report for 1969 notes that budget limitations led to reductions in these programs, outside of CDSC's core on-campus residential courses.[7]

Funding and courses continued at modest levels, below Cold War highs, through the 1970s. Budget data are not available for 1974 to 1995; between 1974 and 1981, course data were available only for 1979. This was a period of churn for the organization and the profession.

Beginning in 1974, there was an effort to reorganize EM functions that was not completed until FEMA was created in 1979. Once that happened, it took at least two years to move CDSC from Battle Creek, Michigan, to Emmitsburg, Maryland, and reorganize it as EMI. President Jimmy Carter created FEMA through a 1979 executive order; when President Ronald Reagan took office in 1981, he put his own stamp on the agency, adding to the period of churn.

After EMI enrolled its first class at the new Emmitsburg campus in 1981, the number of resident courses and graduates trended upward, with a sharp decline during the COVID-19 pandemic, when most courses were offered virtually. Overall, on-campus resident course levels track the number of graduates. See Figures 1.2 and 1.3.

EMI's budget is notably smaller than CDSC's was. The difference might be due to differences in what is counted as part of the EMI budget versus other FEMA entities, such as the closely related National Emergency Training Center (NETC), which manages the Emmitsburg campus. The difference might also reflect a reduction in the number of classified programs or more-technical programs or facilities that were either dismantled after the Cold War or moved elsewhere. Some programs were moved to the Center for Domestic Preparedness (CDP) in Anniston, Alabama, which offers training programs for chemical, biological, radiological, and nuclear hazards.

EMI's post-1995 budget was steadier than it had been in the period before, but there was still year-to-year variation. Notably, the budget does not seem closely related to course or enrollment numbers. Many budget items are for special programs not associated with regular resident courses. EMI is known for its programs on the historical campus in Emmitsburg, but EMI's reach is far greater.

By the 2010s, EMI resident courses were attended by thousands of students per year, and its on-campus facilities, shared with the National Fire Academy (NFA), which operates its own educational program, offered beds for 425. In FY 2022, EMI provided 86 resident course offerings, training 2,379 students on campus in Emmitsburg. The same year, its nonresident programs served 828,848 students, some of whom took multiple courses, for a total of 2,110,403 course completions that year.[8] Nonresident courses include both virtual instructor-led and self-study options.

As of 2022, EMI courses spanned the four phases of EM: mitigation, preparedness, response, and recovery.[9] The courses cover natural hazards (e.g., earthquakes, floods, hurricanes, dam safety), technological hazards (e.g., hazardous material, radiological accidents, chemical accidents), and terrorism. EMI has also offered professional development, leadership, instructional design, public information, integrated EM, and train-the-trainer programs.

Figure 1.4 illustrates EMI activity over time, showing an increase in the number of course offerings and in enrollment. Notably, the EMI-era budget is steadier than the education and training budgets of the CD era, which is explained in more detail in Chapter 3.

---

7 OCD, 1969, pp. 106–114.

8 Senior EMI staff member, email to the author, October 6, 2022.

9 National Training and Education Division, National Preparedness Directorate, FEMA, DHS, "National Preparedness Course Catalog," webpage, undated.

FIGURE 1.2

Number of Resident (On-Campus) Course Graduates, 1951–2021

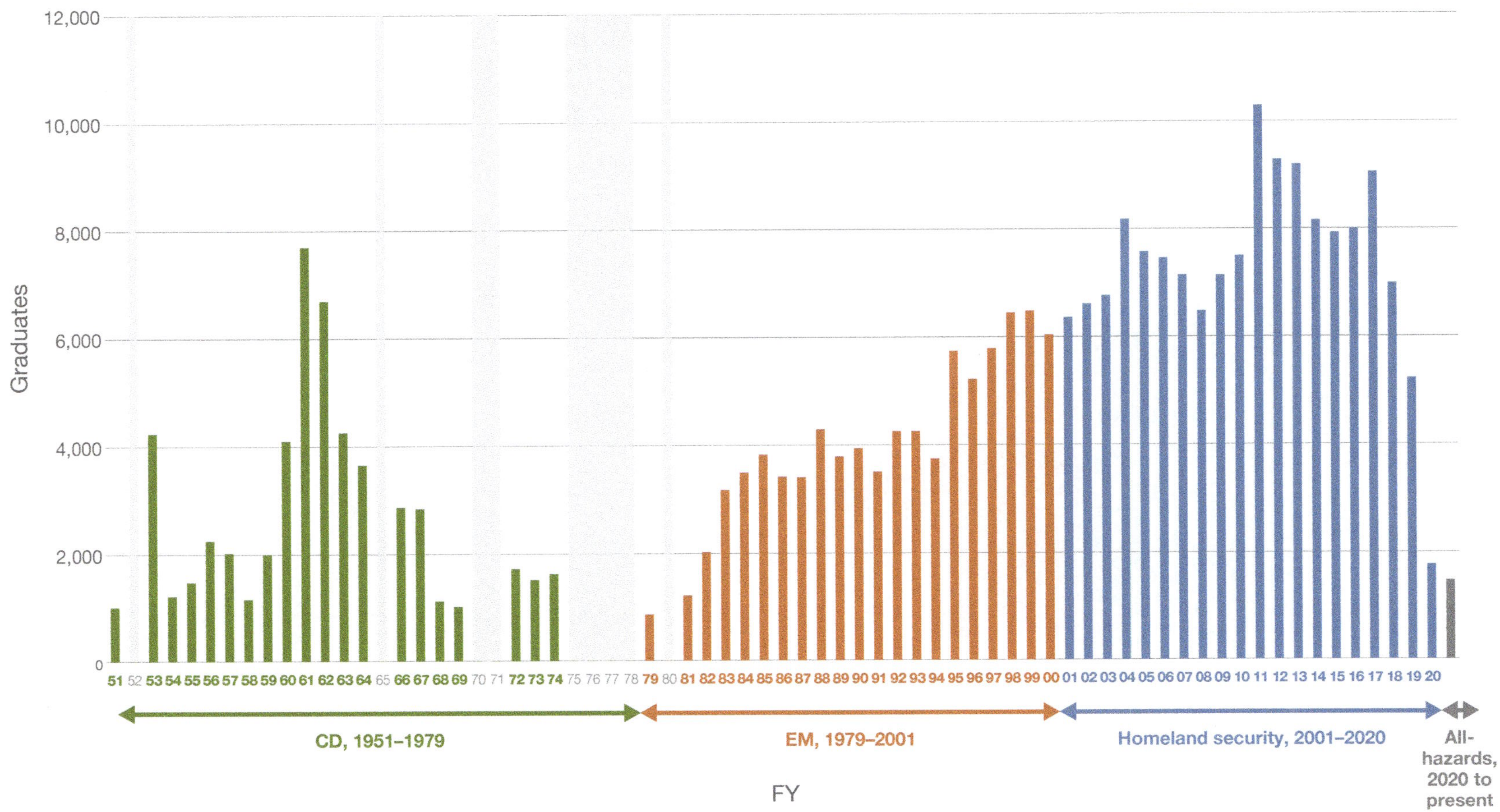

SOURCES: Features data from DCPA, 1972; DCPA, 1974; DCPA, 1975; DHS, 2013; DHS, 2015a; DHS, 2016; DHS, 2017; EMI, *Course Catalog, 1983–1984*, NETC, c. 1983; EMI, *Course Catalog 1984–1985*, c. 1984; EMI, *Course Catalog 1986–1987*, c. 1986; EMI, "1987–88 Schedule of Courses," NETC, c. 1987; EMI, *1988/89 Catalog of Activities*, c. 1988; EMI, *1989/90 Catalog of Activities*, c. 1989; EMI, *Catalog of Activities/1991–1992*, c. 1991; EMI, *Catalog of Activities 1992–1993*, c. 1992; EMI, *Catalog of Activities 1993–1994*, c. 1993; EMI, *Catalog of Activities 1994–1995*, c. 1994; EMI, *Catalog of Activities 1995–1996*, c. 1995; EMI, *Catalog of Activities 1996–1997*, c. 1996; EMI, *Catalog of Activities 1997–1998*, c. 1997; EMI, *Catalog of Activities 1998–1999*, c. 1998; EMI, *Catalog of Activities 1999–2000*, c. 1999; EMI, *Catalog of Activities 2000–2001*, c. 2000; EMI, *Catalog of Activities 2001–2002*, c. 2001; EMI, *Catalog of Activities 2002–2003*, c. 2002; ; EMI, 2008; EMI, 2009; EMI, 2011; EMI, EMI, *Fiscal Year 2012 Training Catalog*, 2012a; EMI, 2012b; EMI, 2013; EMI, 2015; EMI, 2017; EMI, 2018; EMI, 2019a; EMI, 2020; FCDA, 1952; FCDA, 1953; FCDA, 1954; FCDA, 1955; FCDA, 1956; FCDA, 1957; FCDA, 1958; FEMA, 2017; FEMA, 2018a; FEMA, 2019a; FEMA, 2020a; FEMA, 2021a; OCD, 1962; OCD, 1963; OCD, 1964; OCD, 1966; OCD, 1967; OCD, 1968; OCD, 1969; OCDM, 1959; and OCDM, 1960.

NOTE: Gray indicates that I had no data for that year.

FIGURE 1.3

Number of Resident (On-Campus) Courses, 1951–2021

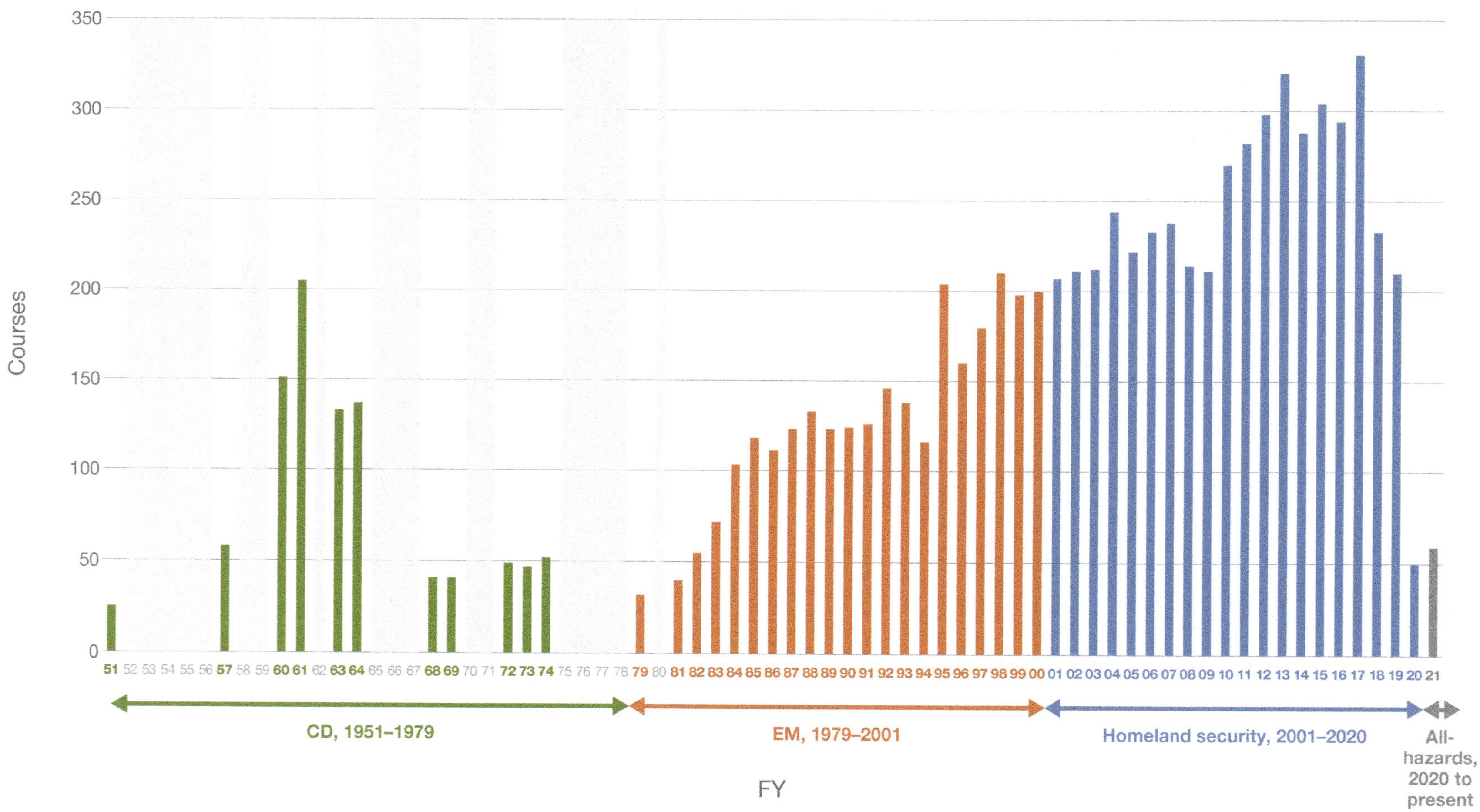

SOURCES: Features data from DCPA, 1972; DCPA, 1974; DCPA, 1975; DHS, 2013; DHS, 2015a; DHS, 2016; DHS, 2017; EMI, 1983; EMI, 1984; EMI, 1986; EMI, 1987; EMI, 1988; EMI, 1989; EMI, 1991; EMI, 1992; EMI, 1993; EMI, 1994; EMI, 1995; EMI, 1996; EMI, 1997; EMI, 1998; EMI, 1999; EMI, 2000; EMI, 2001; EMI, 2002; EMI, 2008; EMI, 2009; EMI, 2011; EMI, 2012a; EMI, 2012b; EMI, 2013; EMI, 2015; EMI, 2017; EMI, 2018; EMI, 2019a; EMI, 2020; FCDA, 1952; FCDA, 1953; FCDA, 1954; FCDA, 1955; FCDA, 1956; FCDA, 1957; FCDA, 1958; FEMA, 2017; FEMA, 2018a; FEMA, 2019a; FEMA, 2020a; FEMA, 2021a; OCD, 1962; OCD, 1963; OCD, 1964; OCD, 1966; OCD, 1967; OCD, 1968; OCD, 1969; OCDM, 1959; and OCDM, 1960.

NOTE: Gray indicates that I had no data for that year.

FIGURE 1.4

The Emergency Management Institute by the Numbers: Annual Trends in Budget, Enrollment, and Courses

The wheel is divided into three eras in EMI's history, which represent different logics: CD, 1951–1979; building the field of EM, 1979–2001, and homeland security, 2001–2020. Data on the annual budgets, number of courses and graduates are incomplete because of gaps in available data, but they do illustrate, at a high level, trends in the history of EMI.

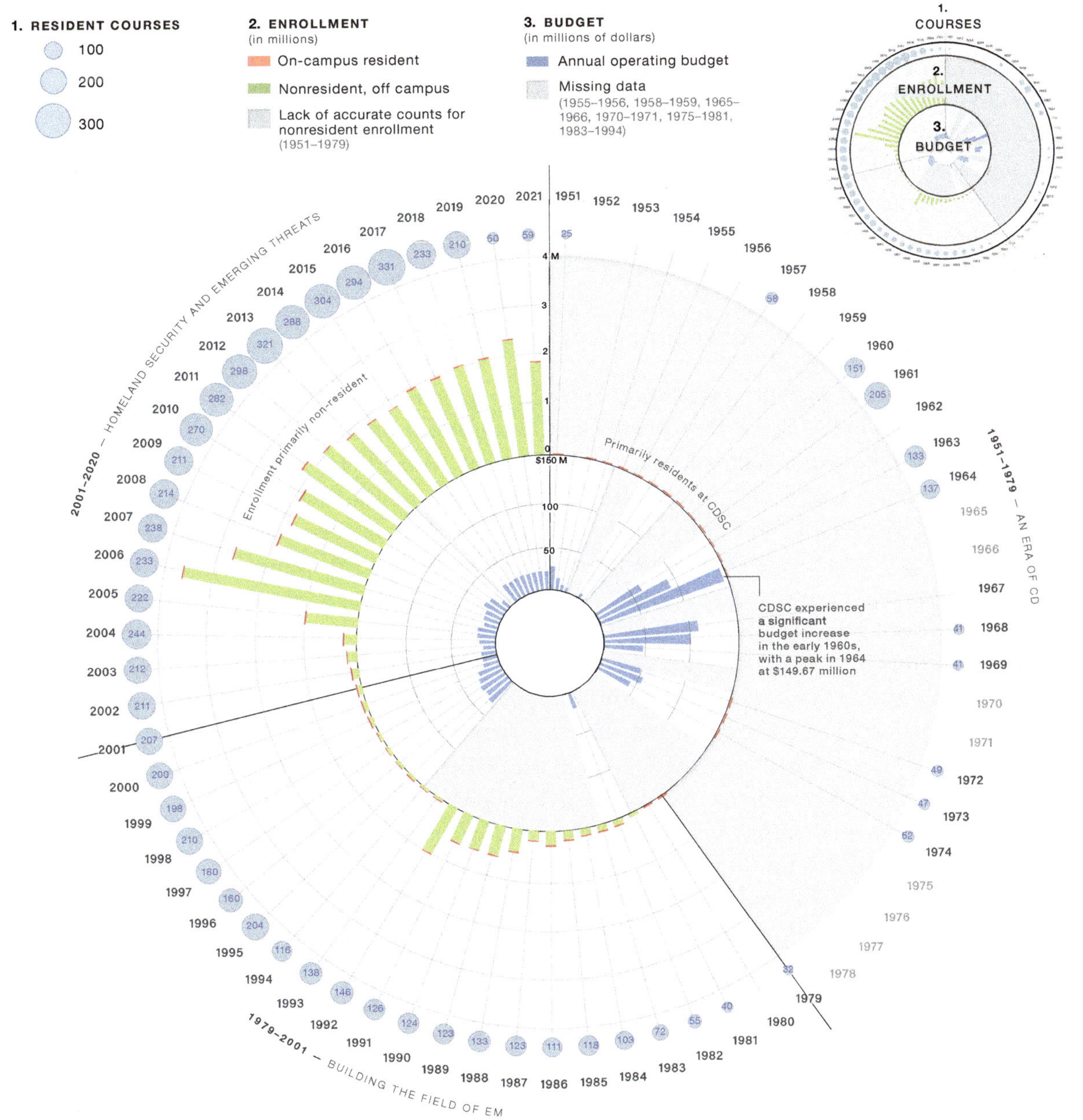

SOURCES: Features information from DCPA, 1972; DCPA, 1974; DCPA, 1975; DHS, 2013; DHS, 2015a; DHS, 2016; DHS, 2017; EMI, 1983; EMI, 1984; EMI, 1986; EMI, 1987; EMI, 1988; EMI, 1989; EMI, 1991; EMI, 1992; EMI, 1993; EMI, 1994; EMI, 1995; EMI, 1996; EMI, 1997; EMI, 1998; EMI, 1999; EMI, 2000; EMI, 2001; EMI, 2002; EMI, 2008; EMI, 2009; EMI, 2011; EMI, 2012a; EMI, 2012b; EMI, 2013; EMI, 2015; EMI, 2017; EMI, 2018; EMI, 2019a; EMI, 2020; FCDA, 1952; FCDA, 1953; FCDA, 1954; FCDA, 1955; FCDA, 1956; FCDA, 1957; FCDA, 1958; FEMA, 2017; FEMA, 2018a; FEMA, 2019a; FEMA, 2020a; FEMA, 2021a; OCD, 1962; OCD, 1963; OCD, 1964; OCD, 1966; OCD, 1967; OCD, 1968; OCD, 1969; OCDM, 1959; and OCDM, 1960.

NOTE: Budgets are inflation-adjusted relative to 2021 dollars. Budget data are not available for 1974 through 1995 or between 1974 and 1981. For 1974 through 1981, course data were available only for 1979. This was a period of churn for the organization and the profession. See the appendix for an extended discussion.

Purpose of This Report

In writing this history, I sought to understand the choices facing decisionmakers involved in the work of CDSC and EMI. I provide context for the environment in which people made key decisions—what options they thought they had available, what tools they had at their disposal, and what stakeholder and other influences were present in their environment. My central research questions were as follows:

- How did EMI evolve along with the professions it served?
- How did CDSC become EMI?
- What eras characterize the history of these organizations?
- What legacy does CD offer EM?
- What were the pivotal events and most-important programs in EMI's history?
- What insights does the history of EMI provide for the institution today and for the EM field?

Report Structure

After the discussion of my analytic approach (Chapter 2), this report is organized chronologically, divided according to major eras in EM. (I use the scholarly term *institutional logics* to characterize the eras. Institutional logics are not logics in the sense of a mathematical proof. Rather, they provide categories to describe a larger rhetorical and institutional environment.) Chapter 3 discusses the first era, CD, from 1951 to 1979. This was the period of CDSC, before FEMA was created. At the beginning, there was enthusiasm for the concept of CD, but budget and strategic commitments waxed and waned—mostly waned. A series of inadequate responses to disasters in the 1960s and 1970s led state and local officials to demand a single federal agency responsible for managing emergencies and disaster relief.[10]

Chapter 4 describes the beginning of the second era, EM, from the creation of FEMA in 1979, and EMI shortly after, to a series of lackluster responses to disasters in the late 1980s and early 1990s that marked a low point for FEMA and marked a turning point for the profession.

Chapter 5 describes the rehabilitation of FEMA's reputation between 1993 and the terrorist attacks of September 11, 2001. During this period, the EM profession developed core concepts and processes and expanded its focus on mitigation, or investing in efforts to reduce the losses caused by disasters. EMI was central to building the profession, as distinct from CD, in states and localities.

Chapter 6 describes the third era, homeland security, from 2001 to 2020. During this period, EMI and the EM profession adjusted to the threat of terrorism and the new DHS, which incorporated FEMA and added a layer between FEMA leadership and the White House. In 2005, Hurricane Katrina refocused attention on natural disasters, and reforms that followed strengthened EM training and career paths.

During that period, the EM profession sorted through new threats, including terrorism, cyberattacks, and, increasingly since 2020, pandemic disease. By the end of the period, EM was called on to manage a diverse array of crises, and the profession wrestled with new responsibilities.

To address these new challenges and responsibilities, EMI sought to expand and update its educational approach topically—through courses in areas that might have been lacking, including logistics and public health—as well as in format—by expanding and modernizing virtual delivery of courses and developing more training and education for senior leaders.

---

[10] Timothy W. Kneeland, *Playing Politics with Natural Disaster: Hurricane Agnes, the 1972 Election, and the Origins of FEMA*, Cornell University Press, 2020; Patrick S. Roberts, *Disasters and the American State: How Politicians, Bureaucrats, and the Public Prepare for the Unexpected*, Cambridge University Press, 2013, pp. 41–75.

Chapter 7 presents my conclusions and my proposal that a fourth era, an expanded all-hazards period, has begun. EM's role in addressing new threats and crises could signal the beginning of an era in which the field must truly prepare for all hazards, using skills in leading across boundaries and crisis management. The field could be at an inflection point. It has gone through transitions in the past, and now is an opportune time to look at EMI's past for insights about how to manage the transition into a new era.

CHAPTER 2

The Analytic Approach and Emergency Management as an Emerging Profession

Summary

This report divides EM history into four eras of institutional logics:

- CD, 1951 to 1979
- EM, 1979 to 2001
- homeland security, 2001 to 2020
- expanded all-hazards, 2020 to the present.

These eras are shorthand for organizing the most-salient threats and hazards, rhetoric, ideas, and policies of each period.

Ideas and policies from earlier eras might fade in importance, but they do not disappear entirely, and they can be drawn on as decisionmakers and other stakeholders face new challenges.

EM is an emerging profession that is developing a body of knowledge and credentials but lacks the gate-keeping function found in some other professions.

To answer the questions posed in Chapter 1, I undertook two research tasks: a review of documents and discussions with current and former EMI staff. In the appendix, I describe these tasks and my methods in detail. The research approach is primarily historical, but historians need criteria beyond a linear chronology to organize material. My approach was to use an analytic framework to organize the history into eras.

The Analytic Framework

Institutional Logics: A Tool for Understanding How Organizations Work and Change

One way to analyze how different eras of EM build on each other is through the concept of *institutional logic*. Institutional logics are "systems of cultural elements (values, beliefs, and normative expectations) by which people, groups, and organizations make sense of and evaluate their everyday activities and organize those activities in time and space."[1]

---

1 Heather A. Haveman and Gillian Gualtieri, "Institutional Logics," *Oxford Research Encyclopedia of Business and Management*, Oxford University Press, January 19, 2017, p. 1.

The logics can be identified through common patterns.[2] In particular, logics have formal rules; enforcement mechanisms, such as law, regulation, or group pressure; and widely accepted informal values, norms, and conventions. Finally, logics are associated with particular audiences and constituencies. Table 2.1 identifies three logics associated with eras in EMI's history: CD, EM, and homeland security. These names were the most–commonly used terms to describe the field associated with the U.S. government's approach to managing crises and emergencies across levels of government (e.g., from national to state and local) during the period. The terms selected for each period are the simplest and most-familiar terms used during that period to describe national-level approaches.

Table 2.1 differentiates the logics according to threats and hazards and forms of organization. The time periods are associated with high-level U.S. government laws and organizations. The CD era ended with the creation of FEMA, and the EM era ended with the creation of DHS.

In the context of EM, the institutional logic approach offers a framework to understand the coevolution of the perceived threats that the United States faces that fall within EM's purview and to characterize how EM institutions organized to respond. The logics exist at multiple levels: within societies, professions, and organizations. Individual emergency managers are embedded in institutional logics, but they also have agency and can leverage multiple institutional logics.[3] Emergency managers interact with their peers, their organizations, and the wider world. These interactions involve *making sense* of the space in which they operate, *evaluating* the threats they face, assigning responsibilities, developing tools to prepare and respond, and developing concepts that *organize* what they do in the face of threats and hazards (i.e., mitigate, prepare, respond, and recover). The characterizations in Table 2.1 summarize general tendencies, described in more detail later in the report.

TABLE 2.1
Comparing Institutional Logics

Institutional Logic	Years	Core Threats and Hazards	Form of Organization
CD	1951–1979	War, nuclear attack	Federal agencies, small state and local offices, volunteers
EM	1979–2001	Fire, flood, hurricane, earthquake, tsunami, radiological or industrial hazard	Small federal agency, grant to a state, locality, or survivor; state or local agency; core emerging profession; NIMS doctrine
Homeland security	2001–2020[a]	Deliberate attack (most salient); terrorism, cyberattack, missile attack; natural or technological hazard; migration	Large federal agency, state or big-city agency, grant to a state or locality, disparate communities within homeland security; composed of multiple fields and professions
Expanded all-hazards	2020–	Natural or technological hazard, deliberate attack, pandemic, cyberattack, climate change, a social problem that impedes societal functioning, such as acute periods of homelessness	Emergency managers as leading across boundaries using informal authorities and incident management skills; emergency managers as trusted brokers

NOTE: NIMS = National Incident Management System.

[a] I considered developments through 2021, but, as discussed in later chapters, the defining characteristics of this era are still emerging.

[2] Trish Reay and Candace Jones, "Qualitatively Capturing Institutional Logics," *Strategic Organization*, Vol. 14, No. 4, November 2016.

[3] Patricia H. Thornton and William Ocasio, "Institutional Logics and the Historical Contingency of Power in Organizations: Executive Succession in the Higher Education Publishing Industry, 1958–1990," *American Journal of Sociology*, Vol. 105, No. 3, November 1999, p. 804; Patricia H. Thornton, William Ocasio, and Michael Lounsbury, *The Institutional Logics Perspective: A New Approach to Culture, Structure, and Process*, Oxford University Press, 2012, p. 2.

Figure 2.1 shows how institutional logics break down across eras with a simple measure of mentions of CD, EM, and homeland security in relevant annual reports and other documents. Mentions of EM outnumber mentions of homeland security in EMI annual reports because EM is at the core of EMI, and other education and training institutions address homeland security. However, *homeland security* appears in EMI annual reports beginning in 2011, and it has a wider impact in the policy space that used to be occupied by EM alone.

The Shift in Institutional Logics Sheds Light on How the Emergency Management Profession and the Emergency Management Institute Have Evolved

CD, EM, and homeland security have different institutional logics, separated in time but overlapping and extending into the present. CD was characterized by a focus on the threat of war, both conventional and nuclear, from abroad. It was organized through a modestly resourced federal effort that attempted to gain buy-in from states and localities and civil society.[4]

Developing out of CD, the EM logic is characterized by a focus on natural hazards, in addition to terrorism and deliberate attack. Functionally, EM takes an all-hazards, all-phases approach, which holds that the best way to manage different kinds of hazards and disasters is to use a similar framework for many kinds of disasters rather than plan for each kind in isolation.[5] The phases of mitigation (reducing losses before a hazard occurs), preparation, response, and recovery characterize this approach, although there have been variations. CD and EM share a focus on identifying vulnerabilities in particular structures or locations and in critical systems that support societal functioning.[6]

The EM logic arose along with the creation of FEMA as an independent federal agency. One of the most-noticeable structural features is that FEMA does not oversee most emergency managers in a hierarchical fashion. Most emergency managers do not work for FEMA and are not compelled to attend EMI to advance in their careers. However, FEMA strongly influences state and local priorities by providing grants, and some of these grants require training provided by EMI (e.g., NIMS training).[7]

The terrorist attacks of September 11, 2001, and the creation of DHS remade the systems for managing emergencies. The homeland security era was characterized by a focus on complex, deliberate terrorist plots originating outside the United States. Over time, new threats, including migration and cyberattacks, appeared on the agenda because of changing threat perceptions and because they fell under the purview of DHS. Natural hazards never went away, but they were incorporated into homeland security logics and often viewed through a security lens.[8] Some of the criticism of the federal response to Hurricane Katrina in 2005 focused on the ways in which homeland security practices distracted from traditional natural-hazard prepa-

---

4 Edward Geist, *Armageddon Insurance: Civil Defense in the United States and Soviet Union, 1945–1991*, University of North Carolina Press, 2019; Andrew D. Grossman, *Neither Dead nor Red: Civil Defense and American Political Development During the Early Cold War*, Routledge, 2002; Roberts, 2013, pp. 41–69.

5 William L. Waugh, Jr., "The 'All-Hazards' Approach Must Be Continued," *Journal of Emergency Management*, Vol. 2, No. 1, 2004.

6 Stephen J. Collier and Andrew Lakoff, *The Government of Emergency: Vital Systems, Expertise, and the Politics of Security*, Princeton University Press, 2021.

7 FEMA, "NIMS Implementation Objectives for Local, State, Tribal, and Territorial Jurisdictions: 2018 Update," c. 2018b.

8 Ryan Ellis, *Letters, Power Lines, and Other Dangerous Things: The Politics of Infrastructure Security*, Massachusetts Institute of Technology Press, 2020.

FIGURE 2.1

The Changing Nature of the Emergency Management Profession, 1979–2019

The shift in institutional logics over seven decades—from civil defense to emergency management to homeland security—sheds light on how the EM profession and EMI's focus have evolved. The wheel figure tracks the count of mentions of *civil defense, emergency management,* and *homeland security* in EMI annual reports and, for 1979 through 1984, EMI-relevant portions of FEMA annual reports.

There is a clear emphasis on CD until the creation of FEMA in 1979. After that, *emergency management* is the most common term until well into the homeland security era. The wheel shows that a growing institutional logic does not make a clean break with the one before. The ideas, rhetoric, and policies at the core build over time, and vestiges of earlier logics remain to be deployed.

PROFESSION TYPE CATEGORY

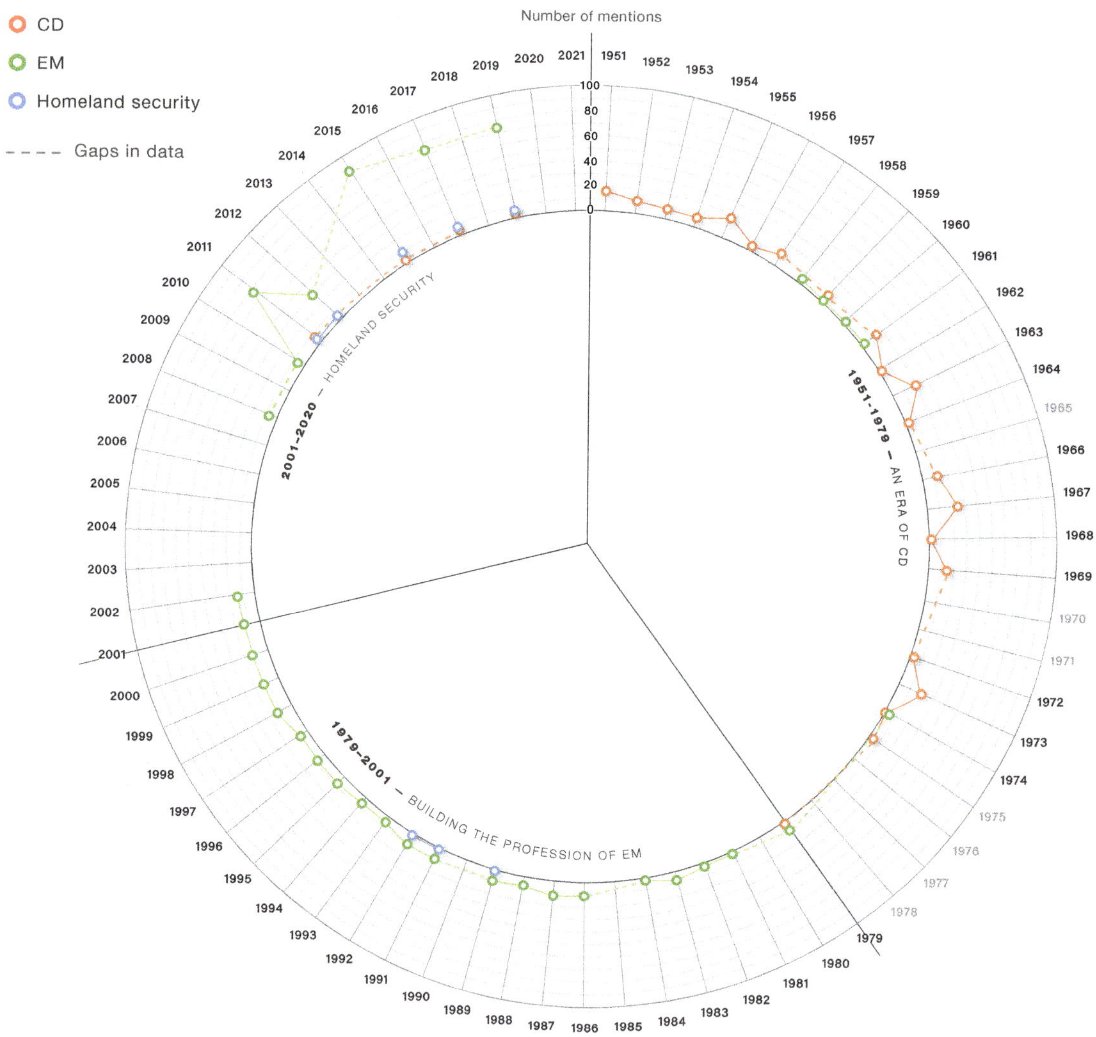

SOURCES: Features information from DCPA, 1972; DCPA, 1974; DCPA, 1975; DHS, 2013; DHS, 2015a; DHS, 2016; DHS, 2017; EMI, 1983; EMI, 1984; EMI, 1986; EMI, 1987; EMI, 1988; EMI, 1989; EMI, 1991; EMI, 1992; EMI, 1993; EMI, 1994; EMI, 1995; EMI, 1996; EMI, 1997; EMI, 1998; EMI, 1999; EMI, 2000; EMI, 2001; EMI, 2002; EMI, 2008; EMI, 2009; EMI, 2011; EMI, 2012a; EMI, 2012b; EMI, 2013; EMI, 2015; EMI, 2017; EMI, 2018; EMI, 2019aEMI, 2020; FCDA, 1952; FCDA, 1953; FCDA, 1954; FCDA, 1955; FCDA, 1956; FCDA, 1957; FCDA, 1958; FEMA, 2017; FEMA, 2018a; FEMA, 2019a; FEMA, 2020a; FEMA, 2021a; OCD, 1962; OCD, 1963; OCD, 1964; OCD, 1966; OCD, 1967; OCD, 1968; OCD, 1969; OCDM, 1959; OCDM, 1960. The data are based on the education and training sections of the annual reports of FDCA, OCDM, OCD, ECPA, and FEMA. For 1986 through 2003, EMI course catalogs were used because annual reports were not available. For 2003 onward, data are from EMI annual reports.

ration and EM.[9] By 2020, however, a focus on long-term emerging threats, including pandemics, cyberattacks, misinformation, civil unrest, and climate change, raised questions about whether a new logic might be emerging.

Homeland security might be the least developed institutional logic because it is the most recent, and historical distance will help future researchers see when it morphed into something else. Some observers might argue that the reforms that followed Hurricane Andrew in 1992 or Hurricane Katrina in 2005 were even more pivotal than the terrorist attacks of September 11, 2001. Although both of these events were catalysts for changes to EM, the reforms drew on many of the basic ideas already present within EM. Homeland security, however, represents a different set of threats and organizations—especially the threat of deliberate attack—and related security issues, including migration, cyberattack, and intrusion.

None of these institutional logics ever disappeared. CD became incorporated into EM and homeland security, like layers of sediment existing underneath new soil. CD logic remains as a resource to be reinvigorated. Between 2018 and 2022, FEMA dusted off old CD plans and updated them in response to the threat of missile attack from North Korea.[10] And the coronavirus disease 2019 (COVID-19) pandemic showed the value of CD-era authorities and practices for national mobilization (including the Defense Production Act), national stockpiles, and logistics. The CD legacy of mobilization could be renewed for the present. More broadly, different institutional logics can be leveraged for different hazards and disasters. EMI's task is to identify which logics and disasters deserve emphasis in its training and education.

Institutional logics exist in the loose confederations that make up the field of EM, and they shape practices in specific organizations, such as EMI. They matter for EMI because they reflect the larger environment in which EMI as an organization operates. CDSC and EMI reflected changes in the larger environment. The tables in this chapter provide a high-level snapshot of changes in the field and emerging professions over time.

The Emergency Management Institute Has Been Shaped by Its Environment

Institutional logics shed light on ideas and practices that became 21st-century EM, but EMI is also a brick-and-mortar organization, led by a director or superintendent for most of its history, with a relatively small staff. In the EMI years, most of the instructors were contractors, not full-time EMI staff, which made hiring cumbersome and gave EMI less control over instructor development than it had over full-time staff development.[11]

EMI has always been part of larger organizations, including several iterations of CD agencies, including FEMA and DHS as a whole. These parent organizations shaped education and training priorities and relationships and set the boundaries for what training organizations could do. The larger group of training and education providers shaped how CDSC and EMI adapted to their niches. This report identifies organizations offering education and training that are most relevant to EMI's mission. College and universities have offered an increasing number of degrees and training programs in EM, often with assistance from EMI. The Naval Postgraduate School serves emergency managers by offering graduate degrees and executive education

[9] Christopher Cooper and Robert Block, *Disaster: Hurricane Katrina and the Failure of Homeland Security*, Times Books, 2007.

[10] Victor Cha and Katrin Fraser Katz, "The Burgeoning North Korea Missile Threat," Center for Strategic and International Studies, April 29, 2022; Dan Vergano, "The US Government Is Updating Its Nuclear Disaster Plans and They Are Truly Terrifying," *Buzzfeed News*, August 24, 2018.

[11] Former senior EMI official, interview 4 with the author, December 17, 2021; senior EMI official, interview 5 with the author, December 17, 2021.

programs in homeland security. Finally, FEMA's CDP is paired with EMI in FEMA's FY 2022–2026 strategic plan in an effort to modernize FEMA's training programs for emergency managers.[12]

Authorities for Emergency Management Span the Emergency Management Institute's Existence

Authorities for education and training have been part of larger authorizations for parent organizations to build the administrative capacity to assist communities before, during, and after disasters. The major authorities for CD and EM training and education are found in the following:

- the Disaster Relief Act of 1950 (Public Law 81-875)
- the Federal Civil Defense Act of 1950 (Public Law 81-920)
- the Robert T. Stafford Disaster Relief and Emergency Assistance Act, Public Law 100-707, 1988, which amended the Disaster Relief Act of 1974, Public Law 93-288
- the Homeland Security Act of 2002 (Public Law 107-296)
- the Post-Katrina Emergency Management Reform Act of 2006 (Public Law 109-295, Title VI).[13]

Before 1950, voluntary organizations, including the American Red Cross and the Salvation Army, provided the bulk of emergency response and recovery support. The 1950 Disaster Relief Act authorized the federal government to provide disaster relief without additional congressional approval.[14] It also allowed the president a means of providing disaster relief through the executive branch, laying the foundation for the growth of administrative agencies, including education and training. Over time, there was redundancy in the administrative processes and organizations that developed to support CD and natural- and technological-hazard EM. CD and EM were on "parallel tracks" through at least the creation of FEMA in 1979, according to one scholarly text.[15] CDSC and EMI balanced serving audiences on both of these tracks.

Each of the authorities listed above shaped EM in fundamental ways, but the Stafford Act is particularly important for EMI. In 2020, EMI's FY 2019 annual report cited Title 6 of the Stafford Act—and none of the other laws—as providing the authority to operate "training programs for the instruction of emergency preparedness officials and other persons in the organization, operation, and techniques of emergency preparedness."[16]

---

[12] FEMA, *2022–2026 FEMA Strategic Plan: Building the FEMA Our Nation Needs and Deserves*, circa December 16, 2021d, p. 21.

[13] Homeland Security Digital Library, "Timeline: Federal Civil Defense Act of 1950," webpage, undated; Public Law 93-288, Disaster Relief Act of 1974, May 22, 1974, as amended, Robert T. Stafford Disaster Relief and Emergency Assistance Act; Public Law 107-296, Homeland Security Act of 2002, November 25, 2002; Public Law 109-295, Department of Homeland Security Appropriations Act, 2007, October 4, 2006, Title VI.

[14] Gary A. Kreps, "The Federal Emergency Management System in the United States: Past and Present," *International Journal of Mass Emergencies and Disasters*, Vol. 8, No. 3, November 1990.

[15] Brenda D. Phillips, David M. Neal, and Gary R. Webb, *Introduction to Emergency Management*, CRC Press, 2012, p. 8.

[16] U.S. Code, Title 42, The Public Health and Welfare; Chapter 68, Disaster Relief; Subchapter IV-B, Emergency Preparedness; Part A, Powers and Duties; Section 5196, Detailed Functions of Administration; Paragraph (f)(1)(A).

Emergency Management Is an Emerging Profession

Throughout EMI's 70-year history, the hazards and threats at the top of the EM agenda have changed, and the field has evolved accordingly. Nuclear war and missile attacks are no longer at the top of the national agenda, although they remain a threat.[17] Concern about natural hazards and disasters increased over time, as did concern about social equity and the ways in which hazards and disasters can have disproportionate effects on marginalized populations. At the same time, some hazards and disasters (e.g., floods) remain constant and pervasive. Ninety-eight percent of counties in the United States have experienced at least one flood event.[18] Still others have appeared on the EM agenda only in the 21st century. These emerging issues include climate change, homelessness, and cyberattacks. Not every emergency manager deals with these emerging issues, but, as more and more do, the field will contend with how to incorporate them. One thing professions do is incorporate new problems and develop standardized processes for addressing them.

CDSC and EMI contributed to the development of their respective professions. This report uses the term *profession* loosely, meaning something more formal than a field. There is no single, widely accepted definition of *profession*, and the professional status of some fields, such as EM, remains disputed. One standard model of professionalization measures the maturity of a profession according to five factors pertaining to when and whether certain milestones have been met:[19]

- the occupation became full time
- training and university programs were established
- national and international associations were established
- state license laws were established
- a code of ethics was established.

By these measures, EM transformed from its CD past and professionalized over time. Table 2.2 gives a sense of when and how EM has professionalized.

EM has longstanding associations and is a full-time occupation, but it lacks bodies that perform a gatekeeping function.

EM can best be described as an emerging, rather than mature, profession.[20] It developed some of the characteristics of professions but did not fully professionalize with the same degree of formality as medicine or law. EMI contributed to an evolving, changing, and emerging profession not primarily by playing a gatekeeper role. Instead, it has been a convener, offering opportunities for newcomers and more-seasoned practitioners to learn about the field, share advice, and grow. The field of EM now has its own journals, associations, body of knowledge, and position titles. EMI has supported the development of elements of a profession within EM while recognizing that the field remains fluid and changing.

---

[17] Timothy M. Riecker, "The Hawaii Saga," *The Contrarian Emergency Manager*, blog post, January 31, 2018.

[18] Leslie Kaufman, Mira Rojanasakul, Hayley Warren, Jason Kao, Brittany Harris, and Prashant Gopal, "Mapping America's Underwater Real Estate: What Happens to Home Prices If Flood Maps Start Measuring Climate Change? Millions of Americans Are About to Find Out," *Bloomberg*, June 29, 2020.

[19] Thomas E. Drabek, "The Professional Emergency Manager: Structures and Strategies for Success," in *The Professional Emergency Manager: Structures and Strategies for Success, Institute of Behavioral Science*, University of Colorado, 1987; Harold L. Wilensky, "The Professionalization of Everyone?" *American Journal of Sociology*, Vol. 70, No. 2, September 1964.

[20] David Farris and Robert McCreight, "The Professionalization of Emergency Management in Institutions of Higher Education," *Journal of Homeland Security and Emergency Management*, Vol. 11, No. 1, 2014.

TABLE 2.2
Emergency Management Professionalization Criteria

Factor	In EM	Year
The occupation became full time	FEMA was created in 1979. Full-time status EM dates in states and localities vary. For example, New York City Emergency Management was created in 1996 under the mayor's office. Prior to that, the function had been combined with other duties.	1979
Training and university programs were established	University of North Texas in Denton, Texas, conferred the United States' first degree in EM in 1983. The degree was a bachelor of science in emergency administration and planning.	1983
National and international associations were established	IAEM was founded in 1952 as the U.S. Civil Defense Council. It was renamed the National Coordinating Council of Emergency Managers in 1985, then renamed IAEM in 1997.[a] NEMA was founded in 1974.[b]	1952, 1974
State license laws were established	This has not occurred.	Not applicable
A code of ethics was established	IAEM and NEMA have codes of ethics for their members, but the organizations' memberships do not encompass the entire profession.[c] A FEMA special interest group was working on a draft code as of 2021, but the code has not been formally adopted.[d]	In development

NOTE: IAEM = International Association of Emergency Managers. NEMA = National Emergency Management Association.

[a] IAEM, "History of IAEM," webpage, undated-a.

[b] Pub. L. 93-288, 1974.

[c] IAEM, "IAEM Code of Ethics and Professional Conduct," webpage, undated-c.

[d] Special Interest Group Working Group on Ethics, FEMA, DHS, "Code of Ethics and Professional Conduct for Emergency Management Professionals," draft under review through December 31, 2021.

History Provides Insight for Planning

The picture of government agencies shaped by larger organizations and a changing threat environment is relevant to EMI as it plans for its future beyond 2022. The FY 2022–2026 FEMA strategic plan calls for EMI to modernize its operational design and "to become the nation's emergency management college."[21] The chapters that follow provide historical context and insights to assist FEMA and EMI in their discussions about modernizing EMI. These include discussions about EMI's internal structure; EMI's relationship to FEMA, DHS, and the rest of the federal government; and its relationship to the profession more broadly. The final chapter addresses indications that EM entered an expanded all-hazards era in 2020 in which it has been given—and continues to receive—responsibility for new kinds of nontraditional missions.

[21] FEMA, 2021d, p. 21.

CHAPTER 3

From Civil Defense to Emergency Management, 1951–1979

Summary

The earliest CD efforts in the United States were a response to the Cold War threats of nuclear attack and invasion.

- CD policy was never fully funded, and CD priorities changed over time. CDSC was an important means through which the federal government communicated CD policy to SLTT civil defenders.
- CDSC was created in 1951. It was a federally funded institution intended to provide short training courses to state and local CD agency officials. The earliest instructors were primarily retired military officers.
- In the early 1960s, CDSC incorporated more chemical, biological, and radiological defense course material and expanded partnerships with higher education institutions, schools, and industry.
- The late 1960s and early 1970s brought an increasing concern about the impact of natural hazards, as well as complex technological incidents, including nuclear and industrial accidents. New course offerings reflected this concern.
- The concept of EM took shape in the 1970s, although training still focused on CD.
- Civil defender was an occupation, but it did not have most of the markers of a profession in terms of formal credentials or degree programs.

CDSC maintained basic continuity over nearly three decades by offering broadly focused courses in administering state and local CD and technical courses in shelter management and radiological protection. However, the waning focus on CD and the growing concern about the toll caused by natural hazards in the latter half of CDSC's history led the college to incorporate more programs related to natural hazards and disasters. The roots of the United States' decentralized approach to EM training lie in the history of CD.

The Civil Defense Staff College Communicates Civil Defense Policy to State, Local, Tribal, and Territorial Governments

CD policy at the federal level shifted over time, and it was never funded to a degree that would permit the policy to be fully implemented.[1] The shifting tides of CD at the federal level mattered because CDSC was where civil defenders at the state and local levels went to learn about what CD was. In an age before the

[1] Geist, 2019.

internet and online tutorials, civil defenders traveled to Battle Creek, Michigan, to learn or traveling teams from CDSC visited SLTT offices to provide training. The federal government used CDSC to inform SLTT partners about what the current CD policy was and how to implement it. Most CD was actually implemented at the SLTT level because it involved protecting the civilian population in case of attack.[2] Implementing CD would be challenging, however, if national-level policy kept changing and if it was never adequately funded. CDSC was put in the tough position of informing SLTT partners about a policy that was frequently changing. Meanwhile, civil defenders faced pressure to prepare for the hazards that were more common in their jurisdictions—whether fires, floods, hurricanes, tornadoes, or earthquakes—rather than for an attack that never seemed to come. Putting CD plans, procedures, and people to best use to prepare for natural hazards was one way in which the federal government received SLTT buy-in to CD.

Civil Defense Policy Priorities Changed over Time

CD policy at a high level shifted as national priorities changed, and CD's changing relationship with the defense community focused on Cold War strategy.[3] During Harry Truman's presidential terms (1945–1953), CD focused on building bomb shelters, which were never adequately funded. Policy shifted in the beginning of Dwight Eisenhower's presidency (1953–1961) to focus on evacuation and then on the building of home fallout shelters. In the John Kennedy (1961–1963) and Lyndon Johnson (1963–1969) administrations, policy shifted again to emphasize community-level fallout shelters rather than backyard home shelters.[4] These community shelters were eventually defunded, but the preference for community shelters remained policy through the 1970s, when attention shifted again to relocating populations in danger of attack. Crisis relocation and evacuation remained policy priorities throughout the Cold War, but efforts to revive and better fund CD in Ronald Reagan's presidency (1982–1984) were not successful, and crisis relocation and evacuation policies were never fully implemented. CDSC was the primary vehicle through which changing national policies were communicated to SLTTs. At the same time, CDSC was tasked with training SLTT officials who also sought support for helping their communities before, during, and after natural hazards and other disasters.

Civil Defense Agencies Reorganized over Time

CD programs were established as part of the peacetime bureaucracy with the onset of the Cold War. The federal government created a CD agency through executive order (EO) and the Federal Civil Defense Act of 1950.[5] The CD bureaucracy went through several names and organizational structures, lasting until the creation of FEMA. CDSC reported to these agencies, which included

- FCDA (1951–1958)
- OCDM (1958–1961)

[2] Frank A. Blazich, Jr., "Accelerated Action: The North Carolina Civil Defense Agency and the Cuban Missile Crisis, October–December 1962," *North Carolina Historical Review*, Vol. 86, No. 1, January 2009; Patrick S. Roberts, "The Lessons of Civil Defense Federalism for the Homeland Security Era," *Journal of Policy History*, Vol. 26, No. 3, 2014.

[3] Geist, 2019.

[4] Donald W. Mitchell, *Civil Defense: Planning for Survival and Recovery*, Industrial College of the Armed Forces, 1966.

[5] Homeland Security Digital Library, undated; Harry S. Truman, "Executive Order 10186: Establishing the Federal Civil Defense Administration in the Office for Emergency Management of the Executive Office of the President," *Federal Register*, December 1, 1950.

- various names and structures, including the Office of Emergency Planning (OEP) and OCD (1961–1972)
- DCPA (1972–1979).

On April 13, 1951, the National Civil Defense Training Center was established in Olney, Maryland. It consisted of a staff college for training in CD management and operations and a rescue school for training in rescue operations.[6] The college and rescue school provided training primarily to state and local agencies. Some other federal agencies also received training, as did some professional associations (e.g., architects, engineers, and educators) and individuals.

Early U.S. Civil Defense Training Followed European Models

CD grew out of efforts to protect populations from wartime attack during World Wars I and II, first in Europe and then in the United States. Many early U.S. CD efforts adopted European models. In its early years, CDSC regularly exchanged personnel with its UK counterpart.[7] The U.S. approach to peacetime CD was more decentralized than the European wartime model, with a relatively small federal bureaucracy delivering training and education to state and local governments, which were to organize their communities.

Civil defenders were primarily state and local officials who provided training and assistance in creating bomb shelters in homes and public buildings. In the event of nuclear war, people would be directed to seek shelter in designated locations and provided with food and water.[8] At the local level, CD directors were usually part-time employees in relatively obscure positions, "located in the county court house basements" according to one EM text.[9] Many of the local CD directors were hired from the military and paid relatively little, in part because they received pensions from the military. At the time, the idea was that the military background would be useful because of the "chaos" that would follow a nuclear attack.[10] Most jurisdictions used civil defenders employed by local government or volunteers as "wardens" who would direct residents to shelters and gas mask repositories. Some CD organizations used volunteer spotters to look for air raids from enemy aircraft.

The Newly Created Civil Defense Staff College Delivered Short Courses for State and Local Civil Defense Officials

The national-level CD organizations coordinated a variety of federal programs to prepare communities for attack and to preserve the continuity of government and key industries in case of attack. CDSC followed a military model, as suggested by the name—it was a site for training members of the CD field. Unlike those in the military, however, most CDSC students did not work for the federal government, and few would advance

---

6 Information Services Office, DCPA, *Significant Events in United States Civil Defense History List Chronologically, 1916–1974*, compiled February 7, 1975.

7 FCDA, 1953, p. 118.

8 Local, State, Tribal, and Federal Preparedness Task Force, *Perspective on Preparedness: Taking Stock Since 9/11—Report to Congress of the Local, State, Tribal, and Federal Preparedness Task Force*, September 2010.

9 Phillips, Neal, and Webb, 2012, p. 6.

10 Phillips, Neal, and Webb, 2012, p. 7; William L. Waugh, Jr., "Shelter from the Storm: Repairing the National Emergency Management System After Hurricane Katrina," *Annals of the American Academy of Political and Social Science*, Vol. 604, No. 1, March 2006.

along a career path that included federal positions. Local civil defense officials provided training to members of their communities, as shown in the example in Figure 3.1.

The college drew enrollments from all states and the territories.[11] Most courses lasted either one or two weeks, and they covered CD administration, evacuation, and sheltering. There were also specialized courses, often in cooperation with other government agencies (e.g., focused on agriculture, schools, or radiological protection).[12]

The central course in the beginning was one week on CD administration provided for mayors, state directors, and city directors of CD.[13] The Federal Civil Defense Act of 1950 provided that the federal government would pay tuition and, for state and local officials, per diem but that the cost of room and board was paid for by employers or participants ($5 per day in 1951).[14] The course provided a picture of the CD threats, beginning with attack from the USSR, assessment of vulnerabilities within a community, and training on how to build community preparedness programs, as well as evacuation and shelter programs.

Courses included hands-on simulation on maintaining city functions in a fictional City X in case of attack. During the simulation, students assumed roles in a city government command post and sent messages to various agencies. The simulation was followed by discussion and analysis of the decisions made. City X was

FIGURE 3.1
Civil Defense Training Ad, Circa 1964

SOURCE: Reproduces an image from Civil Defense Museum, "Civil Defense Art Gallery," webpage, undated-a.

[11] FCDA, 1952, p. 21.

[12] FCDA, 1957, p. 51.

[13] National Civil Defense Staff College, *Training in Civil Defense*, FCDA, 1951.

[14] DCPA, 1975, p. 322.

based on Baltimore, the sixth-largest U.S. city in 1950 and one near multiple military facilities and therefore a potential target.[15]

CDSC was originally located in the Washington, D.C., suburb of Olney, Maryland, along with a rescue school. The rescue school did what its name suggests: It brought students to the campus to simulate rescues, often at night. The school operated a "rescue street" with demolished buildings to replicate conditions after a military attack or natural hazard. Those seeking training would remove simulated casualties or injured people from the building. The 1953 FCDA annual report explained, "Such exercises have demonstrated to civil defense officials and the public the progress that has taken place and how the services work together."[16] The school's leadership attempted to connect its training to an underlying basis in research. The 1952 FCDA annual report notes that the school was "built around scientifically designed American structures simulating wartime damage conditions."[17]

The college also developed courses to inform officials about what federal assistance was available.[18]

The Civil Defense Staff College Fostered Thought Leadership

From the beginning, FCDA and CDSC convened discussions involving researchers about core ideas in the field, an activity that might, in the 21st century, be called *thought leadership*. For example, in June 1951, CDSC brought together outside engineers, CDSC technicians, analysts from the Bureau of the Census, and university researchers to develop a system for determining how much shelter space would be needed in various buildings if there were a nuclear attack.[19] This was not fundamentally a research activity, but it linked researchers with the policy implementers who would design, maintain, and organize sheltering programs.

Some of the thought-leadership activities involved technical communication platforms. For example, in 1951, CDSC hosted a six-day session to discuss building a communication system for CD. The meeting brought together representatives from government and private industry, including representatives from General Electric, Western Union, and American Telephone and Telegraph.[20]

The College Began Operating at Multiple Locations

CDSC was initially located in Olney but moved to Battle Creek in 1954, along with most of FCDA in order to reduce CD agencies' vulnerability to attack, away from the capital.[21] (The administrator and some support staff were in Washington, D.C., and remained after most of the agency moved to Michigan). Most instruction occurred at Olney and, later, Battle Creek. However, CDSC had a "traveling team" as early as 1954 that provided training at federal, state, and local government facilities and at colleges and universities.[22] It also operated several iterations of regional training centers, including an eastern training center in Brooklyn

[15] Eric Stephen Singer, *Saving City X: Planners, Citizens and the Culture of Civil Defense in Baltimore, 1950–1964*, doctoral dissertation, American University, 2012, p. 2.

[16] FCDA, 1954, p. 90.

[17] FCDA, 1953, p. 2.

[18] FCDA, 1957, p. 35.

[19] Information Services Office, 1975, p. 12.

[20] Information Services Office, 1975.

[21] FCDA, 1955, p. 1.

[22] FCDA, 1954, p. 103.

opened in 1958 and a western training center in multiple locations in California beginning in the 1950s.[23] When regional centers periodically closed or shrank, FCDA pledged to link the Battle Creek college more directly to FCDA regions' higher education institutions.[24] After CDSC relocated, the rescue school remained in Olney until it closed in 1958.[25]

The Curriculum Expanded in the 1960s

During the 1960s, CDSC incorporated more chemical, biological, and radiological defense course material and expanded partnerships with higher education institutions, schools, and industry. Overall, however, there was more continuity than change. The course topics were similar to those of the previous decade—managing CD organizations at the state and local levels, shelter management, and radiological protection.[26] In 1963, the most–commonly taught courses were

- CD management
- shelter management for instructors
- CD planning and operations
- radiological monitoring for instructors
- radiological defense offices.[27]

In 1962, CDSC formally incorporated a chemical, biological, and radiological defense school in a new Department of Technical Training.[28] The same year, it also broadened its reach to new partners. It offered "industry defense" courses aimed at building defenses and plans for crucial private industries.[29] The college expanded the number of courses taught at and with colleges and universities, working with 51 institutions in 1964.[30] CDSC also worked with other partners, such as school associations, the U.S. Department of Agriculture for rural area programs, and the U.S. Army for radiological protection.

To broaden its reach to the public, CDSC issued a home-study course in 1969, Civil Defense, U.S.A., offering the basics of CD.[31] After being in operation for nearly two decades, CDSC took strides in professionalizing the field by issuing a pilot "civil defense career development program" for CD coordinators.[32]

The program did not provide a career ladder as much as it provided suggestions for local CD directors to grow in their jobs and motivate their staff, particularly as related to the larger national CD effort. State CD offices offered similar courses.[33]

---

[23] OCD, 1964, p. 58.

[24] FCDA, 1954, p. 56.

[25] Civil Defense Museum, history webpage, undated-b.

[26] OCD, 1964, p. 55.

[27] OCD, 1963, p. 70.

[28] OCD, 1962, p. 62.

[29] OCD, 1962, p. 79.

[30] OCD, 1964, p. 56.

[31] OCD, 1969, p. 106.

[32] OCD, 1969, p. 106.

[33] Iowa Civil Defense Division, U.S. Department of Defense (DoD), *Civil Defense: Training and Education Catalog*, 1974, p. 24.

The Civil Defense Staff College Curriculum Addressed Natural and Technological Hazards

The late 1960s and early 1970s brought an increasing concern for the impact of natural hazards, as well as complex technological incidents, including nuclear and industrial accidents. Some disasters, such as the flooding after a coal mine dam failure in Buffalo Creek, West Virginia, combined both natural hazards and industrial accidents.[34] The bulk of the training still focused on the state and local civil DCPA annual reports, showing a turn toward courses on natural hazards, but the 1973 report emphasized defense against attack.[35]

The push to consider natural hazards came from the Executive Office of the President (EOP) at a time when awareness of environmental impacts was growing in public and political importance. For example, the U.S. Environmental Protection Agency was created in 1970. In 1971, the director of CD in the OEP within EOP, John E. Davis, wrote to Secretary of the Army Robert F. Froehlke,

> My staff and the staff of OCD are working on the details of developing a natural disaster preparedness course for use at the OCD Staff College . . . . I believe this is a worthwhile endeavor and hope we can get it launched in the early future.[36]

In 1972, DCPA and CDSC piloted a course on natural disasters with the OEP (in the White House) aimed at civil preparedness directors throughout the country.[37] EMI also updated the Civil Defense, U.S.A., home-study course to reflect natural hazard information.[38]

A former EMI senior leader recalled that Hurricane Agnes in 1972 was a turning point for the EM field, and a major scholarly account of the event agrees.[39] The hurricane devastated the East Coast of the United States. President Richard Nixon, facing reelection pressure, signed the largest disaster recovery package in history up to that point.

Implementation was slow, however, and survivors blamed the president when red tape slowed the aid. People were confused by the number of agencies involved in providing relief. Journalists during the 1970s were moving from playing "lapdog," in the popular phrase, to "watchdog" and drew attention to the slow delivery of aid with Agnes.[40] The demand for faster and more-organized federal support for states and localities in response to disasters changed the larger environment in which CDSC was operating.

By the 1970s, the term *preparedness* had come into common use to describe what government officials do in preparing for both attacks and natural hazards. Georgiana H. Sheldon, the deputy director of DCPA, said, "Preparedness is the best insurance to meet potential dangers posed by our increasingly complex and technical society. Preparedness today requires the fullest support of all sectors of the community."[41] CD remained a central concept for many people who had spent their careers in the field, but preparedness had arisen as another way to describe what CDSC was educating people to do. Technological threats and hazards were increasingly salient, and they did not always fit a CD mindset because they did not cause deliberate harm.

---

[34] Kai T. Erikson, *Everything in Its Path: Destruction of Community in the Buffalo Creek Flood*, Simon and Schuster, 1976.

[35] DCPA, 1972, p. 21; DCPA, 1974, pp. 19–23.

[36] DCPA, 1972, p. 42.

[37] DCPA, 1972, pp. 25–26.

[38] DCPA, 1972, p. 26.

[39] Kneeland, 2020, p. 2; former senior EMI official, interview 3 with the author, December 13, 2021.

[40] Kneeland, 2020, p. 2.

[41] DCPA, 1972, p. 25.

For example, in 1975, the college developed a course on the fundamentals of planning for nuclear power plant accidents.[42]

The Foundation of Emergency Management Training Took Shape in the 1970s

By the 1970s, support for CD from strategists, Congress, and the public was waning.[43] CD was always underfunded relative to the plans of its proponents. Between 1951 and 1953, President Truman requested $1.5 billion for CD programs, but Congress allocated only $153 million.[44] Funding ebbed and flowed, but it mostly ebbed.

By the 1970s, small programs to support CD shelters and radiological protection monitoring were no match for defending the country against intercontinental ballistic missiles and nuclear war. By the 1970s, the best case for CD against nuclear attack was that it would convince the USSR that the United States was prepared for war—an attitude that was part of the calculus of mutually assured destruction.[45] For its proponents, CD could be a deterrent.

Despite including an increasing amount of course material about natural hazards, CDSC still focused on the subject for which it was named. In 1975, CDSC still offered courses in fallout shelter analysis and radiological protection, and it was developing new cooperative programs with college and university architecture and engineering programs.[46] These modest programs might look farcical in the face of a nuclear war between superpowers and the increasing toll of natural disasters. However, CDSC left its imprint on contemporary EM.

First, it created a precedent for federal involvement in managing emergencies by training state and local officials. CDSC was part of larger federal agencies, often DoD, but it trained primarily state and local government civil servants. It adopted the "college" name, but it neither granted degrees nor trained people in an organization or profession with a clear career ladder as was the case in military staff colleges. CDSC relied on attracting students by getting their buy-in, although most of the students did not pay for training themselves. In addition, colleges and universities became important partners in generating ideas, disseminating knowledge, and encouraging new people to enter the field.

Second, CDSC contributed to a broader national awareness of CD and the threat of attack—and it gave the public something to do in the face of an almost-incomprehensible threat of nuclear war. Historian Laura McEnaney described the accomplishment of CD more broadly as "the graduate encroachment of military ideas, values and structures into the civilian domain."[47] At the same time, state and local officials used what they learned about organizing, sheltering, and evacuation to prepare for tornadoes, hurricanes, floods, and

---

[42] DCPA, 1975, p. 13.

[43] Dee Garrison, *Bracing for Armageddon: Why Civil Defense Never Worked*, Oxford University Press, 2006; Scott Gabriel Knowles, "Defending Philadelphia: A Historical Case Study of Civil Defense in the Early Cold War," *Public Works Management and Policy*, Vol. 11, No. 3, January 2007, p. 219; David F. Krugler, *This Is Only a Test: How Washington, D.C. Prepared for Nuclear War*, Palgrave Macmillan, 2006.

[44] Laura McEnaney, *Civil Defense Begins at Home: Militarization Meets Everyday Life in the Fifties*, Princeton University Press, 2000, p. 25.

[45] Andrew Krepinevich and Barry Watts, *The Last Warrior: Andrew Marshall and the Shaping of Modern American Defense Strategy*, Basic Books, 2015, pp. 47–48.

[46] DCPA, 1975, p. 28.

[47] McEnaney, 2000, p. 6.

other events that were likelier in their jurisdictions.[48] Few state and local officials were focused solely on nuclear attack.

Beyond what it taught about defense against attack, CDSC trained communities and a network of practitioners that communities should not expect the federal government to rescue them.[49] Schools were important to CDSC because they could send the message to parents that communities and households needed to prepare themselves.[50] CDSC programs made community-level preparedness programs central to how the United States prepared for emergencies of all kinds. The structure of national preparedness was broadly similar between the CD era and EM, but much changed between the periods, too.

---

48 Roberts, 2014, pp. 354–383.

49 McEnaney, 2000.

50 Grossman, 2002.

CHAPTER 4

Building the Field of Emergency Management, 1979–1992

Summary

FEMA was created after requests from governors and localities for a better-coordinated federal approach to disaster relief.

- CDSC was renamed EMI and moved to Emmitsburg, Maryland, following the creation of FEMA in 1979.
- Technological emergencies, such as the Three Mile Island nuclear meltdown, showed that EM could be used for more than natural hazards.
- Scandals in 1984 and 1985 distracted from EMI's work.
- EMI helped make the all-hazards idea become more widely known in the 1980s.
- EMI contributed to building a nascent profession during this period. The EM education and training ecosystem grew in the 1980s.
- EMI contributed to the field by convening thought leaders.

President Carter's EO 12148 created FEMA on July 15, 1979, by consolidating disparate disaster relief and preparedness programs. This seminal moment in EM history created a focal point for federal programs and ideas, concepts, and doctrine about how to prepare for, respond to, and recover from disasters. The move of CDSC to Emmitsburg and the change in name and focus to EMI punctuated the transition from CD to preparedness for a variety of hazards and emergencies in a nascent profession.

One impetus for the creation of FEMA was states' and localities' frustration with the lack of a central federal entity responsible for disaster relief. A 1978 National Governors' Association report documented governors' increasing concern about "the lack of a comprehensive national emergency policy, as well as the dispersion of federal responsibilities among numerous federal agencies, which has hampered states' ability to manage disaster situations."[1] The report and meetings held in the preceding year affirmed support for comprehensive EM as a core idea for a new agency. *Comprehensive EM* referred to the idea that EM should link the federal government, states, and localities. It also organizes EM according to four functions: mitigation, preparedness, response, and recovery. (These would later be referred to as *phases* in a *cycle*.)

Local governments also called for a new agency. A survey by the International City/County Management Association for FEMA indicated that many cities lacked emergency organizational structure, had dormant EM programs with minimal budgets, had plans that had not been received or updated for a long time, and lacked EM training and exercises.[2] FEMA reported the results of the survey as motivation to build EMI.

---

1 National Governors' Association, *1979 Emergency Preparedness Project: Final Report*, 1979, p. ii.

2 FEMA, "Welcome to the National Emergency Training Center," FEMA-12, October 1981, p. 5.

The creation of FEMA and the move away from CD was not without detractors. Some advocates of CD were concerned that the change would diminish the United States' preparedness for confrontation with the USSR.[3] Debates over how to reorganize and then how to implement President Carter's EO creating FEMA (EO 12148) slowed the transition from CDSC to EMI.

Formally, the effort to create FEMA began as one part of the Carter administration's reorganization project, an effort to streamline government services.[4] President Carter ran out of time to pursue comprehensive legislation, so he issued an EO using reorganization powers that the presidency possessed at the time.[5] The reorganization addressed many of the complaints of states and localities about the objections of federal agencies that stood to lose programs to new agencies. The process was rushed, according to a National Academy of Public Administration report, but it resulted in a new agency focused on EM.[6] President Carter emphasized the new agency's potential to have synergies in preparation and response for multiple hazards and disasters, and he made mitigation central to the new agency: "We want to bring together for the first time programs aimed at preventing and mitigating the effects of potential national disasters, such as floods and fire, with those designated to deal with these disasters once they occur."[7]

The Emergency Management Institute Is Moved into the Federal Emergency Management Agency and Opens a New Campus

After FEMA was established in 1979, CDSC was transferred from DoD to FEMA and became EMI, reflecting a new focus on all-hazards EM. On March 6, 1979, FEMA purchased Saint Joseph College in Emmitsburg for $3,514,000 and renamed it NETC.[8] NETC was officially dedicated on October 8, 1979. EMI, along with NFA (part of USFA) moved to the NETC campus.[9]

The Emmitsburg Site Was Chosen by Committee and Politicians' Input

Emmitsburg was not the first location considered for EMI. The search began well before FEMA was created, with a search for a site for a new fire academy after publication of the 1973 National Commission on Fire Prevention and Control report, *America Burning*, that cautioned that "the richest and most technologically advanced nation in the world leads all the major industrialized countries in per capita deaths and property loss from fire."[10] The following year, President Gerald Ford signed the Federal Fire Prevention and Control

[3] "High-Level Jousting over Civil Defense," *Washington Post*, June 19, 1978.

[4] John R. Dempsey, "Carter Reorganization: A Midterm Appraisal," *Public Administration Review*, Vol. 39, No. 1, January–February 1979.

[5] Analyst in American national government, *Presidential Reorganization Authority: History, Recent Initiatives, and Options for Congress*, Congressional Research Service, R42852, December 11, 2012.

[6] Gary L. Wamsley, *Coping with Catastrophe: Building an Emergency Management System to Meet People's Needs in Natural and Manmade Disasters*, National Academy of Public Administration, 1993, pp. 14–15.

[7] Jimmy Carter, "Federal Emergency Management Agency Remarks Announcing Reorganization Plan No. 3 of 1978," June 19, 1978a.

[8] USFA, *U.S. Fire Administration 25th Anniversary: Challenging Fire in America for 25 Years*, 1999, p. 4.

[9] EMI, 2020, p. 6.

[10] National Commission on Fire Prevention and Control, *America Burning: The Report of the National Commission on Fire Prevention and Control*, 1973, p. 1.

Act of 1974.[11] The act directed the Secretary of Commerce to appoint a site-selection board that would make recommendations for a new fire academy site based on a range of options from, at the lower end, minimal activity and limited direct training of fire service personnel to, at the higher end, an expanded level of instruction, including on-campus facilities and room to grow.[12]

The board received proposals from 223 sites, and it quickly narrowed that group to 140. To further narrow the options, the board used the following criteria:

- minimal acquisition and refurbishment cost
- sufficient existing facility
- immediate availability
- accessibility to a major airport
- location appropriate for a national academy, with cultural and support services and a national image.

The board decided that the academy needed space for on-site instruction, and these criteria helped the board narrow the options to 13. It ranked Marjorie Webster Junior College in Washington, D.C., as its first choice and Saint Joseph College in Emmitsburg as its second and submitted both options to the Secretary of Commerce in July 1976. The board found that the main distinction between the two sites was travel distance to Washington, D.C.

In May 1977, Marjorie Webster Junior College was purchased with the belief that the facility contained 100,000 square feet of space and required a $2.4 million renovation. In an architectural study, these figures were found to be incorrect, which led to a year of deliberation and revisiting of other sites. Meanwhile, members of Congress promoted sites in their district, and Senator Paul Sarbanes advocated on behalf of the former Saint Joseph College site in his Maryland district.[13] However, according to one news article, the White House made the final site-selection decision.[14] Ultimately, on March 24, 1979, Saint Joseph College was purchased to serve NFA.[15]

The Emergency Management Institute Had Greater Input into the National Emergency Training Center Campus in the Past but, Since 1993, Has Been a Tenant

During the period in which a site for NFA was selected, a parallel process resulted in the creation of FEMA from formerly disparate disaster assistance programs. USFA was moved into FEMA, with the logic that fire was one of many hazards for which the new FEMA would prepare. However, USFA maintained its own distinctive culture and organizations. EMI and NFA shared space on the Emmitsburg campus but had different reporting chains. NFA would report through USFA, while EMI sometimes reported through training branches within FEMA.

[11] Public Law 93-498, Federal Fire Prevention and Control Act of 1974, October 29, 1974.

[12] John L. Swindle, Henry D. Smith, and David M. McCormack, *Report of the National Academy for Fire Prevention and Control Site Selection Board*, National Fire Prevention and Control Administration, U.S. Department of Commerce, 1976.

[13] "Maryland Site Gets Nod for Academy," *International Fire Chief*, Vol. 45, No. 3, March 1979, p. 4.

[14] "Maryland Site Gets Nod for Academy," 1979, p. 4.

[15] Michael Hillman, "A Short History of St. Joseph College," Emmitsburg Area Historical Society, webpage, undated.

Throughout most of its history, NFA managed the Emmitsburg site, known as NETC. However, in at least one brief period, EMI had greater control over the site. According to a former senior EMI official, after approximately 1990, FEMA created an Office of Training, which included NFA and EMI. Laura Buchbinder, who served as EMI superintendent from 1987 to 1993, was dual-hatted, also serving as director of FEMA's Office of Training.[16] However, some in the fire community wanted to "reunite" NFA with USFA, and, in the early 1990s, EMI was made a tenant of NETC, which was managed by USFA.[17] On September 7, 1993, FEMA administrator James Lee Witt wrote a memo summarizing changes intended to achieve a "consolidation of functions, centralized management and administrative systems, and all-hazards operational capability, and equitable distribution of resources." This included a reorganization that gave USFA oversight over the NETC campus, which included EMI.[18] Prior to this time, FEMA leadership, rather than USFA, one level down in the FEMA organization chart, oversaw the NETC campus.

NFA reported through USFA between the creation of DHS in 2003 through creation of DHS's Preparedness Directorate. In 2007, EMI was moved out of the Preparedness Directorate layer and out of USFA's jurisdiction.[19] USFA continued to manage the NETC campus, however, and EMI had to work closely with NFA on campus-related matters.

The Curriculum Changed with the Move to Maryland

EMI's move from Michigan to Maryland from 1979 to 1981 was accompanied by a shift in curriculum that put natural-hazard preparedness on the same plane as CD. EMI and the NETC campus were established to provide training and education that would lead to "reduced loss of life and reduced damage to property" in a variety of hazards and disasters.[20] According to a FEMA brochure, the new NETC was created to prepare for emergency in "times of peace and times of war" and natural or "modern technological" hazards, likely referring to the Three Mile Island nuclear meltdown.[21]

Many of the staff who moved to Emmitsburg had already incorporated natural hazards into their courses. CDSC and EMI staff member Peter Vogel recalled,

> Actually most of us were very, very happy about the idea of the move. It was exciting. And what were really excited about, more than just the physical move from Battle Creek to Emmitsburg, was we were excited about having a broader mission to work with. We were very centric to nuclear war, and nuclear war preparedness. But the real bread and butter of emergency management wasn't that. Most of us knew it was floods and tornadoes and earthquakes, hazmats, plane crashes, train wrecks, whatever.[22]

---

[16] Former senior EMI official, email to the author, September 27, 2022.

[17] Former senior EMI official, email to the author, September 27, 2022.

[18] "Witt Reinvents FEMA," *Natural Hazards Observer*, No. 2, November 1993, p. 3.

[19] EMI was transferred out of USFA's jurisdiction as part of the Department of Homeland Security Appropriations Act, 2007 (Pub. L. 109-295, 2006) (Subcommittee on Technology and Innovation, Committee on Science and Technology, U.S. House of Representatives, *The United States Fire Administration Reauthorization: Addressing the Priorities of the Nation's Fire Service*, hearing, 110th Cong., 1st Sess., October 2, 2007).

[20] FEMA, 1981, p. 5.

[21] FEMA, 1981, p. 5.

[22] Pete Vogel and Shane Gibbon, *EMI 60th Anniversary*, DVD, EMI, 2011.

The period from 1978 to 1982 was a relatively slow time for training because of the transition to the new FEMA organization. Budget and course offerings were lower in these years than in the years before or after, and some data were never reported, as described in the next section.

By 1982, estimated enrollment was 87,000 students.[23] The majority of students were state and local officials, including fire chiefs, police captains, water and sewage directors, and planners. Among the federal attendees were officials responsible for radiological protection, design, and assessment.[24]

Most instructors were hired through individual contracts rather than being permanent staff. The instructor pool was drawn largely from state officials who were experts in a course's subject matter, state or local leaders of emergency exercises, college and university professors, or experts from federal labs.[25] A curricular review and advisory committee shaped the curriculum based on the perceived needs of the EM profession rather than those of CD. Specific hazards and disasters were linked by comprehensive and integrated approaches to EM involving mitigation, preparation, response, and recovery.[26] Participants in EMI training came from many of the same diverse EM-related fields from which CDSC students came, at all levels of government, although the majority were from local agencies.

New Course Content Focused on Emergency Response

Course content was intended to provide "integrated training," multiagency response, and mitigation, according to an early report from the agency.[27] EMI inherited CD courses from its predecessor, CDSC. These courses covered such topics as how to prepare for and respond to radiological events and attack. At the same time, the new EMI was intended to chart a course for the field of EM.

In 1980, EMI held a series of seminars to dissect what could be learned from a variety of disasters and how FEMA might help: the San Diego aircraft collision in 1978, the Wichita Falls tornado in 1979, the eruption of Mount Saint Helens in 1980, and a fire at the MGM Grand Hotel in Las Vegas in 1980.[28] In addition, the group analyzed the 1980 riots in Miami. The riots led to at least 18 deaths and $100 million in property damage. Notably, these types of events command headlines four decades later, although some hazards and disasters for which emergency managers have been given responsibility in recent years are missing. These newer hazards include pandemic disease, cyberattacks, active shooters, homelessness, migration, and opioid abuse.

In 1981, 47 EM experts met in Emmitsburg to map the subjects that should be covered in EMI's programs.[29] The group included federal, state, and local officials and faculty from colleges and universities. Federal officials came from the National Oceanic and Atmospheric Administration, the National Weather Service, and the U.S. Geological Survey. The group also included state water resource program representative, and college search-and-rescue leaders. There were few scholars of EM at the time, so the group was made up primarily of experts in EM's contributing fields and disciplines.

---

[23] FEMA, 1981, p. 6.

[24] FEMA, 1981, p. 6.

[25] FEMA, 1981, p. 10.

[26] FEMA, 1981, p. 13.

[27] FEMA, 1981, p. 7.

[28] FEMA, 1981, p. 7.

[29] Peter L. Smith and Joseph M. Bishop, *Proceedings of the Natural Hazards Management Seminar*, Emergency Management Institute, February 23–27, 1981, c. 1981.

The participants found a lack of understanding of how authority flowed in these crises, a lack of command-and-control procedure, a poor understanding of roles, poor communication, and a "piecemeal" response.[30] The same criticisms could be made of more-contemporary emergencies, perhaps including pandemic and cyberattack response.

Figure 4.1 shows how the group divided the field according to a mix of organizations, topics, and disaster phases.

FIGURE 4.1

Model of the Emergency Management Field from a 1981 Emergency Management Institute Seminar

ORGANIZATIONAL MODEL

FEDERAL	REGIONAL	STATE	LOCAL	INSTITUTIONAL	INDIVIDUAL
AGENCIES	AGENCIES	AGENCIES	GOVTS	INSTITUTIONS GROUPS FAMILIES	INDIVIDUALS

TOPICAL MODEL

EARTH	WIND	FIRE	WATER
EARTHQUAKE	TORNADO	FIRE	RIVERINE FLOOD
LANDSLIDE	HURRICANE		COASTAL FLOOD
SUBSIDENCE	EROSION		ICE JAM
VOLCANO			WINTERSTORM
			MUDSLIDE
			COASTAL EROSION
			TSUNAMI
			DROUGHT

DISASTER PHASE MODEL

PRE-DISASTER	WARNING	READINESS	RESPONSE	RECOVERY
PLANNING	WARNING SYSTEMS	STAFFING	OPERATIONS	ASSESSMENT
AWARENESS	COMMUNI-CATIONS			MITIGATION

CRITIQUE

19

SOURCE: Reproduces an image from FEMA, 1981, p. 7.

30 FEMA, 1981, p. 7.

One of the first courses offered at EMI was on disaster recovery operations. The course covered how to run a disaster assistance center and how to manage crisis communication—topics not generally covered at CDSC, according to Bruce Marshall, an EMI instructor during that period.[31]

The Emergency Management Institute Explored New Organizational Models with a Civil Defense Imprint

EMI's creation gave rise to discussions among the then–relatively small EM community about what kind of organization should it be—a degree- or credit-awarding institution? A train-the-trainer program? A developer of doctrine? The fact that *institute* appears in its name does not answer these questions. At the time EMI was created, military staff colleges trained general officers and were explicitly charged with doctrine formation.[32] Neither of these applied to EMI. The term *institute* referred to a higher education institution with a more applied technical focus. The term persists in the 21st century, as in the Massachusetts Institute of Technology and Virginia Military Institute.

Although EMI provided applied technical training, it also served as a convener. EMI portrayed its role as bringing together groups that might normally be "turf oriented" to have a productive discussion: police and fire, CD, emergency medical service, and public works.[33] FEMA administrator Louis Giuffrida, who served from 1981 to 1985, proposed that colocating fire and EM training in Emmitsburg could help overcome those divisions.[34]

As a focal point for a new profession, EMI had an opportunity to set the gold standard for EM education. Former FEMA associate director for training and education Fred J. Villella framed EMI's goal as maintaining quality.[35] In practice, he sought quality by seeking external approval for NFA courses first. By 1981, 18 NFA courses were accredited by the American Council on Education, but FEMA did not report any accreditation for EMI courses, perhaps because EMI was in the process of transitioning to its new organizational model in Emmitsburg. Some colleges and universities provided credit for student work at EMI, however. For example, Michigan State University issued credit equivalences for some courses, allowing them to be earned as part of a Michigan State degree, although it is not clear how many people used EMI courses formally as credits toward a degree. EMI was created to serve the CD and EM professions, but the demand for higher education credentials in the field was unclear in 1981 and potentially less than the demand in the fire services field.

Villella and Giuffrida both joined FEMA after serving in a California state-level organization that tended toward the CD side of the spectrum, the California Specialized Training Institute (CSTI). As governor, Ronald Reagan had asked Giuffrida to leave the Army to serve as the inaugural director of CSTI and provide advice on counterterrorism.[36] Giuffrida served as CSTI director until he was appointed by then-president Reagan as FEMA administrator.

CSTI provided training in EM and CD, and it provided counterterrorism and counterriot training to police. California of the 1960s and 1970s saw high-profile terrorist activities (e.g., the Weather Underground)

---

[31] Vogel and Gibbon, 2011.

[32] Robert A. Doughty, *The Command and General Staff College in Transition, 1946–1976*, CGSC, June 11, 1976.

[33] FEMA, 1981, p. 7.

[34] FEMA, 1981, p. 7.

[35] FEMA, 1981, p. 7.

[36] Ronald Reagan, "Nomination of Louis O. Giuffrida to Be Director of the Federal Emergency Management Agency," February 24, 1981.

and concern about civil unrest (e.g., protests driven by racial or ethnic divides). The law enforcement training and concern about riots, terrorism, and civil unrest at the time in California provided more of a security emphasis to CSTI than many other state-level EM and CD training programs had.

Giuffrida and Villella brought the culture of CSTI to the newly created EMI. Some of EMI's early curriculum designers came from CSTI, according to EMI staffer Marshall.[37] The integrated EM course also had its origins in CSTI, according to Marshall. The security culture of CSTI was carried over to the early years of EMI through its leadership, although not all of the staff shared the perspective of FEMA and EMI leaders.

EMI staff worked to bridge the CD and EM cultures. A 1983 FEMA report portrayed EMI's mission in its early years as "dialogue and role definition" among the various groups that make up EM, such as police, fire, emergency services, and public interest groups.[38] These dialogues stressed response to disasters more than mitigation or recovery.

The Emergency Management Institute Searched for Its Niche

EMI was not the only entity within FEMA to provide training. FEMA's training and education (under various names over the years) also provided training to agency staff, and FEMA's regions provided training to states in mitigation, preparedness, response, and recovery.[39] States, localities, and nonprofits provided their own training, sometimes working with FEMA and even using EMI materials and sometimes conducting training independently or with other partners.

Given this large set of training providers, EMI had to identify what it could do better than or differently from other trainers and educators. EMI had a national reach, and it could reach beyond FEMA to the full EM community. As a federal institution, EMI represented federal, whole-of-nation goals. It also had funding to pay for state and local officials' travel and per diem costs to attend training. And it was dedicated to EM.

At a planning workshop bringing together stakeholders in EMI, FEMA's training and education division framed EMI's role as a convener: EMI provides a national forum for discussion conferences for selected "Federal, State, local, and private sector audiences."[40] EMI could also distinguish itself in providing more hands-on and applied courses than were common in the universities. For example, many of EMI's instructors had practiced EM or CD as managers or leaders. Some might have had other primary roles and professions, such as in policing or fire, but their professional experience usually included some connection to emergencies and crisis management.

As part of this applied focus, exercise and scenario-based learning techniques were a "cornerstone" of EMI's approach, according to former superintendent Stephen Sharro, and part of EMI from the beginning.[41] To some degree, higher education more broadly is adopting approaches that were present at EMI's origins. Project-based learning is becoming more common in higher education because it stimulates social learning through small groups and provides an opportunity to apply theory to practice.

In EMI's first few years, FEMA trainer Albert H. Fluman worked with roughly 50 emergency managers from around the country to develop and conduct exercise-based training courses. Fluman took learning objectives from classroom-based courses and designed exercises to meet those objectives.[42]

---

[37] Vogel and Gibbon, 2011.

[38] FEMA, *Report from the Training and Fire Programs Directorate*, 1983.

[39] Smith and Bishop, 1981, pp. 31–32.

[40] Smith and Bishop, 1981, pp. 31–32.

[41] Stephen Sharro, "How EMI Trains for and Responds to Disasters," *911 Magazine*, March–April 1995, p. 45.

[42] Vogel and Gibbon, 2011.

EMI put forth a long-term goal of "setting in motion a training methodology or system that will be self-perpetuating at the state or local levels so that once a priority has been developed, the state or community can adopt it and tailor it to local needs."[43] EMI could not direct states and localities to adopt its concepts or training methods, but it could convene stakeholders, coordinate, and lead from behind. One of the largest divides with which EMI contended at its founding was between two groups that might appear to outsiders to be similar: civil defenders concerned about nuclear attack, and emergency managers focused on natural hazards.

The Federal Emergency Management Agency Navigated Between Civil Defense and Natural Hazards as Context for the Emergence of the Emergency Management Institute

Although FEMA was responsible for preparing for a variety of hazards and emergencies, the choice between whether to focus on CD against attack or natural hazards presented a stark alternative. After taking office in 1977, President Carter ordered a review of the federal approach to CD.[44] The review led President Carter to issue Presidential Directive (PD) 41, "U.S. Civil Defense Policy," in 1978 to shore up CD and provide a new rationale. The revitalized CD program was to "enhance deterrence and stability" and reduce the possibility for coercion. This new purpose stands in contrast to earlier rationales for CD as insurance in case deterrence failed.

Discussions about how to structure FEMA were tied up with debates about how to implement PD-41 in a timely fashion.[45] CD as enhanced deterrence was composed of two general categories of activity that fell under the heading of "mobilization": evacuation planning and other programs should a crisis occur, and construction and maintenance of shelters.

Practical realities stood in the way of full implementation. By the late 1970s, the utility of evacuation as CD was in question. The United States was not spending nearly enough to provide shelter for the full population from nuclear attack. And given the speed of attack and potential scale of nuclear war, full evacuation appeared impossible.[46]

By the mid- to late 1970s, national security policymakers had reached the conclusion that Soviet CD efforts "could not remotely alter the strategic balance," that U.S. deterrence was not harmed by Soviet CD efforts, and that a very expensive U.S. CD program was not warranted.[47] By 1979, a DCPA analysis portrayed CD programs at roughly $100 million a year as "paper plans only."[48]

In retrospect, one option might have been to move more swiftly from CD to EM and natural hazards. At the time, however, FEMA had a mandate to prepare for CD, rooted in the Federal Civil Defense Act of 1950 and the more recent PD-41. Many of the people and programs that made up FEMA were focused on CD and maintained a commitment to preparing for attack, whether the rationale was insurance or deterrence.

As a practical matter, FEMA could not shift too far away from natural hazards without putting programs at risk. In 1977, the Office of Management and Budget (part of EOP) sought to "kill" programs that were

---

43 FEMA, 1981, p. 18.

44 William Lanouette, "The Best Civil Defense May Be the Best—or Worst—Offense," *National Journal*, September 9, 1978.

45 William Chipman, *Civil Defense for the 1980's: Current Issues*, DCPA, white paper, July 13, 1979, p. 53.

46 Chipman, 1979, p. 36.

47 Les Aspin, "The 'Mineshaft Gap Revisited: Soviet Civil Defense and U.S. Deterrence," unpublished manuscript, December 1977; Chipman, 1979, p. 33.

48 Committee on Banking, Housing, and Urban Affairs, U.S. Senate, *Civil Defense*, hearing on oversight on the role of civil defense in the United States–Soviet strategic balance, the effectiveness of existing Soviet and U.S. programs, and the feasibility of passive defenses for the survival of the population and the economy, 95th Cong., 2nd Sess., January 8, 1979, pp. 51–53.

not focused on preparedness for attack on the ground: "readiness for peacetime disasters is not a federal concern."[49]

By 1980, following PD-41 and a renewed emphasis on deterrence in the Reagan administration, the plan appeared to maintain a "seed for a nucleus for a cadre to develop CD capabilities on a rapid-mobilization basis."[50] Activities included shelter surveys, crisis relocation planning, evacuation planning, and radiological defense. The seed idea meant that CD programs were to maintain sufficient capacity that they could be rapidly expanded in a year if the threat environment required it.

FEMA balanced CD and natural-hazard concerns by returning to the principle of dual use, the idea that plans and programs could be used for preparedness for both attacks and natural hazards. Civil defenders and state and local officials expressed concern that the balance between the two might tilt too far in one direction or the other.[51]

PD-41 struck a balance for dual use by emphasizing preparedness for attack, but providing that "Civil Defense programs should also help deal with natural hazards and other national emergencies." Questions remained among officials at all levels of government about the federal commitment to CD.[52] Would the federal government support or even require states and localities to take meaningful action to prepare for attacks? Or would CD become empty rhetoric? EMI programs to train state and local officials were a key test of what *dual use* meant in practice.

Three Mile Island and Technological Emergencies Posed New Challenges

PD-41 was one outcome of a long debate in Congress and policy circles about the need for a single disaster agency that combined preparedness for attack and natural hazards. An accident at the Three Mile Island nuclear plant in 1979 drew attention to a new kind of emergency: complex technological accidents. Although no one died in the accident, it was the most serious accident at a nuclear plant in U.S. history, and it exposed gaps in managing nuclear emergencies—in particular, poor inter- and intragovernmental coordination and poor communication.[53]

FEMA was created by EO before the accident. However, it was not authorized to respond to radiological emergencies.[54] Evacuation planning had been DCPA's responsibility, but evacuation of the region surrounding Three Mile Island was never ordered.[55]

The Three Mile Island meltdown showed that EM skills and concepts could be put to use for novel incidents. EM involves coordination and communication among agencies, not just filing formal hazard mitigation plans before an incident and evacuation plans after. The accident was what public policy scholars call

49 Chipman, 1979, p. 67.

50 Chipman, 1979, p. 55.

51 Chipman, 1979, p. 66.

52 Chipman, 1979, p. 66.

53 President's Commission on the Accident at Three Mile Island, *Report of the President's Commission on the Accident at Three Mile Island—The Need for Change: The Legacy at TMI, October 1979, Washington, D.C.*, Pergamon, 1980; Mark Stencel, "A Nuclear Nightmare in Pennsylvania," *Washington Post*, March 27, 1999.

54 FEMA, *Three Mile Island Generating Station Exercise: April 14, 2009*, June 19, 2009, p. 3.

55 Subcommittee on Military Installations and Facilities, Committee on Armed Services, U.S. House of Representatives, *Civil Defense and the Three Mile Island Nuclear Accident: Report of the Military Installations and Facilities Subcommittee of the Committee on Armed Services*, 96th Cong., 1st Sess., December 18, 1979, p. 6.

a *focusing event*:[56] It focused attention on the need for planning for technological accidents. Many disasters had the quality of focusing events, leading to public attention and political reform. However, not all disasters automatically lead the public to focus over a sustained period of time or lead to reform. What counts as a focusing event is determined after the fact. And in many cases, threats and hazards emerge at the top of the agenda because different groups mobilize around them. The environmental movement—not just the event itself—contributed to an awareness of technological hazards and industrial accidents.

After the Three Mile Island meltdown, a presidential commission recommended that FEMA be given responsibility for planning for nuclear accidents and reviewing relevant facility plans.[57] On December 7, 1979, the president directed FEMA to assume responsibility for civilian nuclear planning and response, and, in 1980, FEMA and the Nuclear Regulatory Commission signed a memorandum of understanding to divide their responsibilities.[58]

The Emergency Management Institute and Civil Defense in the 1980s: What Counts as a Disaster?

EMI's new name raised the issue of defining *emergency* and *disaster*. A growing social science community interested in disasters addressed the question in an attempt to define the most-important concerns. In a famous essay, sociologist Enrico L. Quarantelli posed the question, "What is a disaster?" His work spawned a wide variety of theoretical and practical answers.[59] Most of the literature that followed focused on the level of harm to people and the environment and on the acute nature of the event, as opposed to chronic conditions, such as poverty. Ultimately, however, scholars did not agree on what counted as a disaster. Some events, such as a tornado or a hurricane, were clearly disasters for which emergency managers would have to prepare. Yet there was no consensus about other events. If no people died but nature was affected, was it still a disaster? Many experts thought that a weather event without consequences for people was just part of nature's cycle of renewal, no matter how strong the winds, high the flood waters, or hot the fire.

The field settled on the idea that certain concepts or practices were common across disasters but that some kinds of disasters might be qualitatively different from others. Preparation, response, and recovery apply to all disasters, and most kinds of disasters can be mitigated in advance. Quarantelli warned that, despite the commonalities, all disasters are not the same:

---

56 Thomas A. Birkland, "Focusing Events, Mobilization, and Agenda Setting," *Journal of Public Policy*, Vol. 18, No. 1, January–April 1998.

57 President's Commission on the Accident at Three Mile Island, 1980, p. 76.

58 Code of Federal Regulations, Title 44, Emergency Management and Assistance; Chapter I, Federal Emergency Management Agency, Department of Homeland Security; Subchapter F, Preparedness; Part 350, Review and Approval of State and Local Radiological Emergency Plans and Preparedness; Code of Federal Regulations, Title 44, Emergency Management and Assistance; Chapter I, Federal Emergency Management Agency, Department of Homeland Security; Subchapter F, Preparedness; Part 351, Radiological Emergency Planning and Preparedness; Code of Federal Regulations, Title 44, Emergency Management and Assistance; Chapter I, Federal Emergency Management Agency, Department of Homeland Security; Subchapter F, Preparedness; Part 352, Commercial Nuclear Power Plants: Emergency Preparedness Planning; Jimmy Carter, "President's Commission on the Accident at Three Mile Island Remarks Announcing Actions in Response to the Commission's Report," December 7, 1979c; FEMA and U.S. Nuclear Regulatory Commission, "Memoranda of Understanding Between Federal Emergency Management Agency and Nuclear Regulatory Commission," *Federal Register*, Vol. 45, No. 243, December 16, 1980; Office of Standards Development, Founding U.S. Nuclear Regulatory Commission, *Regulatory Guide*, Vol. 88, 1985.

59 Ronald W. Perry, "What Is a Disaster?" in Havidan Rodriguez, Enrico L. Quarantelli, and Russell R. Dynes, eds., *Handbook of Disaster Research*, Springer, 2006; Ronald W. Perry and E. L. Quarantelli, eds., *What Is a Disaster? New Answers to Old Questions*, Xlibris, 2005.

> [I]f people are asked to evacuate from a certain area, whether the impetus for the evacuation is radiation fallout or a hurricane doesn't matter. However, people are only going to accept certain warnings as legitimate. But fundamentally, we thought that a nuclear attack was qualitatively different from any other situation. Therefore, we could not say to what degree the response to a nuclear attack or a hurricane would be similar.[60]

The field as a whole, and FEMA's training and education programs in particular, settled on an approach that moved from a specific-service orientation (e.g., fire, policing, health, or public works) toward thinking of multiple services or offices that support the field of EM.[61] EM coalesced around the idea that the field was linked through phases of activity: mitigation, preparedness, response, and recovery. All were common to multiple kinds of hazards. Expertise in these phases constituted the core of EM, and it allowed the field to claim expertise in managing an unlimited number of emergencies because the core knowledge was not about the hazard or threat itself but about the phases of the disaster cycle. Emergency managers differed from hydrologists, for example, because they had expertise useful in multiple kinds of disasters.

The phased approach was known in various guises, including integrated EM and comprehensive EM. One FEMA report noted that "comprehensive emergency management spans the full spectrum of emergencies from local disasters to nuclear war and extends through all levels of government and the private sector."[62] *Integrated EM* referred to a series of topics related to the roles, responsibilities, materials, and resources needed to manage the phases of an emergency.[63] An alternative view was that EM should focus on root causes and underlying vulnerabilities. Although integrated EM never displaced the phased approach, an understanding of social vulnerability was integrated into EMI courses related to disaster science.[64]

One step forward for integrated EM was a 1981 amendment to the Federal Civil Defense Act that allowed the use of CD funds for peacetime disaster, as well as attack preparedness, along with the proviso that the effort "[be] consistent with, contribute[] to, and . . . not detract from attack-related civil defense preparedness." Within a few years, however, that proviso was "largely ignored," according to one analyst, and CD funds were used for natural-hazard preparedness.[65]

The Emergency Management Education and Training Ecosystem Emerged in the 1980s

EMI both influenced and was influenced by education and training outside of the institute. EMI regularly reviewed college and university course syllabi to assess the state of knowledge in EM.[66] EMI did not assume that EM concepts originated from Emmitsburg or even from FEMA headquarters in Washington, D.C., in a top-down manner. Rather, teachers and scholars refined the concepts in the field and experimented with

---

[60] Enrico L. Quarantelli, "The Origins and Impact of Disaster Research," in Margaret R. O'Leary, ed., *The First 72 Hours: A Community Approach to Disaster Preparedness*, iUniverse, 2004, p. 322.

[61] FEMA, 1983, p. 4.

[62] FEMA, 1983, p. 1.

[63] FEMA, 1983, p. 1.

[64] Lee Bosher, Ksenia Chmutina, and Dewald van Niekerk, "Stop Going Around in Circles: Towards a Reconceptualisation of Disaster Risk Management Phases," *Disaster Prevention and Management*, Vol. 30, No. 4–5, 2021.

[65] William K. Chipman, "Putting the 'DUAL' Back into Dual-Use Civil Defense," *Journal of Civil Defense*, June 1989, p. 13.

[66] Wayne Blanchard, "Compilation of Outlines and Syllabi of Emergency Management–Related College Courses," EMI, May 25, 1995.

new ideas, and EMI leadership found that the best way to keep abreast of the evolving field was reviewing course syllabi.

Practically, much of the training for the field occurred outside of EMI, in states and localities. Between 1982 and 1984, FEMA delivered more resources to regional offices and gave the regions more of a role in coordinating training.[67] Perhaps in response, EMI emphasized train-the-trainer programs.[68] These had always been part of CDSC's menu of approaches to CD, but FEMA and EMI materials show that these programs received a new emphasis in the 1980s. EMI would not train all emergency managers, but it could train many of the trainers who would themselves interact with local emergency managers and related government agency and nonprofit leaders.

Some people in western states complained that traveling to Emmitsburg for training was too much of a burden. One former senior EMI official recalls being sent to Carson City, Nevada, to determine whether it would be a suitable location for a proposed EMI West.[69] According to a former senior EMI official, plans for an EMI West were derailed by scandal and turnover in EMI.

FIGURE 4.2
An Emergency Management Class, 1987

SOURCE: Reproduces an image from EMI, 1987, p. 45.

[67] FEMA, 1983, p. 5.

[68] FEMA, 1983, p. 4.

[69] Former senior EMI official, interview 2 with the author, December 13, 2021.

FIGURE 4.3
An Emergency Management Class, 1987 or 1988

SOURCE: Reproduces an image from EMI, 1987, p. 11.

Despite the distance some would travel, state and local officials praised EMI's courses. See Figures 4.2 and 4.3 for images of EMI classes during the 1980s. California representative George Edward Brown, Jr., praised EMI's integrated EM program as a step forward in developing "a multihazard research, planning and mitigation approach to deal with emergencies."[70] In 1984, Los Angeles mayor Tom Bradley brought 60 staff members to Emmitsburg for training to prepare Los Angeles for a variety of disasters, including terrorism, civil unrest, and earthquakes. He praised EMI's classroom instruction and exercises for highlighting areas for improvement and building "camaraderie" among city departments that do not always talk to one another. Bradley embraced the all-hazards focus of EM (an integrated approach to emergency preparedness) that the "lessons learned cover any kind of emergency, under any circumstances, including the Olympics."[71] Los Angeles would host the summer Olympics four months later.

The Emergency Management Institute Contributed to a Social Science Thought-Leadership and Research Community

Aside from offering resident training courses and offsite, or nonresident, courses, EMI contributed to building the core concepts of the profession, an activity that would later be called *thought leadership*, to use a term coined in 1994.[72] The institute reached the highest levels of the profession, and it linked state and local elected officials with EM concepts and their staffs who worked on EM issues. In 1983, EMI began its first training program for state EM directors.[73] At least as early as 1984, EMI offered an integrated EM course for mayors.[74]

---

70 George E. Brown, Jr., "Mayor Tom Bradley Attends the Federal Emergency Management Agency's Integrated Emergency Management Course," *Congressional Record*, Vol. 130, Part 7, April 25, 1984.

71 Evan Maxwell and Bill Farr, "Disaster Strikes Los Angeles: This Is a Test," *Los Angeles Times*, March 9, 1984.

72 John Hall, "Is Thought Leadership Everything It's Cracked Up to Be?" *Forbes*, November 3, 2019.

73 FEMA, 1983, p. 4.

74 FEMA, 1983, addendum 1.

Thought-leadership activities extended to the university environment. EMI's NETC campus housed the Senior Executive Policy Center (SEPC), which was originally a panel of university leaders (primarily deans) designed to introduce the idea of EM into graduate and undergraduate public administration curricula. The SEPC group, led by Dean Charles Bosner (Indiana University Bloomington) and William Petak (University of Southern California), intended to introduce the field of EM to the Network of Schools of Public Policy, Affairs, and Administration (then called the National Association of Schools of Public Affairs and Administration). Approximately 30 people met at NETC in 1984 to learn more about EMI and FEMA. The group included a variety of disciplines, such as public administration, planning, policy science, urban planning, and public policy.[75]

The group met first at FEMA headquarters in Washington, D.C., then spent two weeks in Emmitsburg at the EMI campus, shown in Figure 4.4. Some had studied hazards and disasters for years or even decades. Louise Comfort was an expert on earthquake policy, Beverly Cigler studied local government management of hazards, and Richard Sylves wrote a book on the Nuclear Regulatory Commission's role in managing risk. William Waugh researched terrorist attacks. Others, however, were new to the study of hazards and disasters. The group met with FEMA personnel and disaster scholars, primarily sociologists associated with the Disaster Research Center at Ohio State University (now at the University of Delaware). Notably, members also made a site visit to Three Mile Island.[76]

In 1984, the group produced a special issue of *Public Administration Review* devoted to the new field of EM. The special issue became a seminal framework for EM as a part of the public administration field, and several of the issue's articles have been cited more than 500 times.[77] The group reflected the link between EM, CD, and preparedness for civil unrest and terrorism. The group sponsored a terrorism seminar with high-visibility speakers, including special counsel to the president Edwin Meese III.[78] Meese had worked with FEMA administrator Giuffrida and FEMA executive deputy director Villella in California, and Meese was instrumental in bringing the two to FEMA.[79]

Waugh and Goss tracked this group (those at the SEPC/FEMA/EMI meeting) and found that it formed the core of the disaster research community.[80] Between 1984 and 2012, the group produced 22 books, more than 120 peer-reviewed articles, and 78 book chapters. They directed 17 doctoral dissertations and received grant funding of approximately $7.8 million. Members of the group also testified before Congress and contributed to the development of the Certified Emergency Manager (CEM) program and EM sections of their professional disciplines. The CEM program is the primary credentialing program for the field.

[75] William L. Waugh, Jr., and Kay C. Goss, "The History of Higher Education in Emergency Management: The Emergency Management Institute, the National Science Foundation, and the William Averette Anderson Fund," *Journal of Emergency Management* (Weston, Mass.), Vol. 17, No. 1, January–February 2019.

[76] Louise K. Comfort, William L. Waugh, and Beverly A. Cigler, "Emergency Management Research and Practice in Public Administration: Emergence, Expansion, and Future Directions," *Public Administration Review*, Vol. 72, No. 4, July–August 2012.

[77] For example, David McLoughlin, "A Framework for Integrated Emergency Management," *Public Administration Review*, Vol. 45, January 1985, and William J. Petak, "Emergency Management: A Challenge for Public Administration," *Public Administration Review*, Vol. 45, January 1985.

[78] FEMA, 1983, addendum 1.

[79] Howard Kurtz, "Retired Military Policemen Troop into Highly Paid Agency Jobs," *Washington Post*, February 3, 1985.

[80] Waugh and Goss, 2019.

FIGURE 4.4
The Emergency Management Institute Campus

SOURCE: Reproduces an image from EMI, 1983, p. 4.

Emergency Management Institute Scandals Led to an Institutional Reboot

In 1984 and 1985, a series of scandals among FEMA leadership involving the NETC campus where EMI was located led to a period of soul-searching as EMI looked for new leadership. The institute's civil servants continued to train and educate emergency managers and innovate—for example, delivering video courses. Nevertheless, the public attention shaped views of EMI during this period.

Federal and congressional investigators uncovered evidence of cronyism and the misuse of funds within FEMA and NETC (the EMI campus) that led to the resignation of the FEMA associate director and eventually the administrator.[81] Representative Al Gore of Tennessee, the chair of the Subcommittee on Investigations and Oversight, Committee on Science and Technology, U.S. House of Representatives, found "an extensive pattern of misconduct and mismanagement at the highest levels" of FEMA.[82]

The issues can be divided into two buckets: one concerning special favors and the misuse of funds, focusing on NETC's education and training and the other concerning the use of the NETC campus. FEMA and EMI political appointees, not career civil servants, were the focus.

The House subcommittee's investigation focused on NETC and found that "[t]he evidence . . . indicates that favors and gratuities may have been provided by some contractors to top FEMA officials, and, it looks as though in return, special treatment may have been provided to contractors."[83] Some FEMA leaders were reported to have used sole-source contracts to employ friends.

At NETC, the committee investigated allegations about over-the-top campus renovations, including a gourmet pizza oven, a fireplace, expensive fixtures, and a full-time chauffeur for leadership of the campus that housed EMI. There were also allegations of cronyism in hiring and sexual harassment. Villella, the FEMA associate director for training and education who supervised NETC, resigned during the investigation. After the year-long investigation, the House panel recommended that the U.S. Department of Justice investigate FEMA, including potential perjury by the FEMA administrator, Giuffrida, over allegations of waste, fraud, and abuse that included EMI but went well beyond it to other FEMA activities.[84] Giuffrida resigned in 1985 before the investigation could take place.[85]

The scandals affected EMI in at least three ways: First, the scandals consumed time and attention that could have been used to develop new initiatives and grow EMI. Investigations required staff to prepare reports in response, and one staff member recalled that new initiatives fizzled out because of the distraction.[86] Villella was the top appointee overseeing EMI, and, by 1984, he was in the spotlight for allegations that he misused the campus, including renovating the campus chapel for his daughter's wedding.[87]

Second, the scandals might have contributed to EMI's reputation as disconnected from other FEMA activities. At the time, EMI had a reputation as a "turkey farm." When someone in FEMA headquarters wanted to get rid of someone, they would send them to the "turkey farm," which referred to the NETC campus in Emmitsburg.[88]

Finally, the scandals might have accelerated EMI and FEMA's move away from CD. Giuffrida and Villella emphasized FEMA's national security and CD responsibilities in preparing the United States for missile and nuclear attack from abroad and preserving the continuity of government in case of attack. Both had military backgrounds, and Giuffrida, a former Army lieutenant colonel, was known at FEMA as "the general."[89] Many of their efforts emphasized CD or counterterrorism. Their focus reflected the Reagan administration's priori-

---

[81] Kurtz, 1985.

[82] Subcommittee on Investigations and Oversight, Committee on Science and Technology, U.S. House of Representatives, *Oversight: Federal Emergency Management Agency*, 98th Cong., 2nd Sess., October 24, 1984, p. 297.

[83] Subcommittee on Investigations and Oversight, 1984, p. 297.

[84] "A House Panel Has Recommended That the Justice Department . . .," United Press International, July 26, 1985.

[85] "Head of Disaster Relief Agency, Targeted in Inquiries, Resigns," *Los Angeles Times*, July 25, 1985.

[86] Former senior EMI official, interview 2 with the author, December 13, 2021.

[87] Subcommittee on Investigations and Oversight, Committee on Science and Technology, U.S. House of Representatives, *Oversight: Federal Emergency Management Agency*, 99th Cong., 1st Sess., March 4, 1985, p. 36.

[88] Jerry Strope, "Scandal Strikes at FEMA," *Journal of Civil Defense*, October 1984, p. 5.

[89] Kurtz, 1985.

ties. With their resignations and FEMA and EMI searching for a new direction, CD was without two of its most prominent advocates.

Funding and resources for CD waned in the second Reagan term (beginning in 1985) because of declining support for CD. Rather than fund CD, strategists favored spending to increase the U.S. military strength in an attempt to lead the USSR to increase *its* defense spending to a level that would harm its economy.

The Concept of All-Hazards Was Institutionalized in the 1980s

The scandals at FEMA and EMI led to the resignations of champions of CD and left room for the proponents of a more natural hazard–focused approach to enumerate the disasters for which EM should prepare. The closure of DCPA and the creation of FEMA in 1979 marked the beginning of the institutionalization of the all-hazards approach to EM, rather than the CD approach that privileged preparation for nuclear war. Although Giuffrida and Villella drew attention to FEMA and EMI's CD and counterterrorism education roles, by 1985, their departure left room for a greater focus on all hazards.

The all-hazards approach provided a unifying framework to describe what EM is, beyond a collection of specific plans for very different kinds of disasters. The idea, formerly known as "all risks," was presented in the 1979 National Governors' Association report that led to the creation of FEMA.[90] All-hazards provides a framework for managing hazards across all four phases: mitigation, preparation, response, and recovery. It also recognizes that processes for managing hazards have much in common and can be approached with the same core set of skills and plans. This approach contrasts with a CD mindset that focuses on a particular threat of attack and with other approaches that emphasize specific plans, skills, and expertise for different kinds of disasters. By the mid- to late 1980s, EMI annual reports reflected the focus on all hazards, describing the approach as mitigating, preparing for, responding to, and recovering from "any and all disastrous situations which hit your jurisdiction."[91]

With the decline of CD and the disruption at EMI, all-hazards became institutionalized (that is, considered routine and embedded formally in organizational structures and documents[92]) at EMI and in the profession more broadly. Using the concept of all-hazards in EMI reports and training helped spread the concept to emergency managers throughout the country. Professional associations also adopted the concept and shifted toward EM during the 1980s. For example, IAEM began as the U.S. Civil Defense Council, its name from 1952 to 1983. It became the National Coordinating Council on Emergency Management in 1983 and was renamed IAEM in 1998.[93]

CD programs were not always shuttered immediately. Sometimes they were combined with all-hazards approaches to reducing disaster losses, as shown in FEMA annual reports about training and education from the 1980s and other training materials. In one pair of case studies performed for FEMA, a manufacturing company and a service delivery company planned for alternative sites in case of disruption by either threat-

---

[90] IAEM, "Principles of Emergency Management Supplement," September 11, 2007; National Governors' Association, 1979.

[91] EMI, c. 1987, p. 2.

[92] Cynthia Hardy, "How Institutions Communicate; or How Does Communicating Institutionalize?" *Management Communication Quarterly*, Vol. 25, No. 1, 2011; John W. Meyer and Brian Rowan, "Institutionalized Organizations: Formal Structure as Myth and Ceremony," *American Journal of Sociology*, Vol. 83, No. 2, September 1977.

[93] Roberts, 2013, p. 93.

ened attack (i.e., CD) or natural hazards (the all-hazards idea).[94] Relocation plans supported preparation for both CD and natural disasters.

EMI officials reported as late as 1990 that nuclear exchange was a central hazard but that some emergency managers "didn't even want to come in to take those types of courses at the time."[95] Demand from SLTTs pulled EMI toward all-hazards and away from CD as much or more as the push from EMI itself did. A series of natural disasters drew public attention to what some perceived as a slow response from the federal government.[96] When Hurricane Hugo caused approximately $7 billion in damage along the East Coast in 1989, public attention shifted to natural hazards.[97]

Sharro served as EMI deputy superintendent from 1990 to 2000 and as superintendent from 2000 to 2006. He said that Hugo was a turning point for elected officials to pay attention to EM agencies at all levels of government: "Hurricane Hugo highlighted the role of elected and appointed officials in disasters and emergencies," Sharro said. "The bigger the incident, the more important parts they play. So, we expanded EMI's audience to include mayors, city managers, department heads, coroners/medical examiners, etc."[98]

---

94 James M. O'Donnell and James V. Zaccor, *Organizational Relocation Plan Development: Two Case Histories*, Industrial Emergency Council, April 1985.

95 Former senior EMI official, interview 4 with the author, December 17, 2021.

96 Bill McAllister, "FEMA Officials Admit Response to Hugo Was Slow," *Washington Post*, October 6, 1989.

97 National Weather Service, "Hurricane Hugo—September 21–22, 1989," webpage, undated.

98 Stephen Sharro, "Leadership in a Time of Great Change," EMI, 2021.

CHAPTER 5

The Federal Emergency Management Agency's Reputation Restored: The James Lee Witt Era, 1993–2001

Summary

Under Witt's leadership, FEMA and EMI improved their reputations, which had been damaged by scandals.

- EMI added a new mission: training the FEMA disaster-response workforce.
- FEMA developed international reach as EMI developed support for programs at the end of the Cold War. One large initiative helped countries from the former USSR clean up and dispose of fissile material.
- EMI expanded the train-the-trainer approach, training trainers throughout the country for students who might not be able to attend EMI courses.

By 1992, FEMA's reputation was at a low point. After a series of disasters in the late 1980s and 1990s, including Hurricane Andrew in 1992, FEMA's response was judged to be insufficient and too slow. There were questions about the efficacy of its mitigation programs. Recovery programs were minimal. When former Arkansas governor Bill Clinton became president in 1993, he appointed his state emergency services director as FEMA administrator. The appointment was a watershed for the profession because it marked the first time a county- or state-level EM director had been appointed to lead FEMA.

Witt's leadership of FEMA from 1993 to 2001 brought a turnaround of the agency's reputation in the eyes of the public and political leaders and a renewed focus on the agency's core natural-hazard mission. At the same time, the Witt-led reorganization reduced the emphasis on national security programs that required security clearances, such as programs to maintain continuity of government in case of attack. The agency also added a customer service focus to improve the experience of people preparing for or affected by disasters.[1]

[1] R. Steven Daniels and Carolyn L. Clark-Daniels, *Transforming Government: The Renewal and Revitalization of the Federal Emergency Management Agency*, PricewaterhouseCoopers Endowment for the Business of Government, April 2000; R. Steven Daniels and Carolyn L. Clark-Daniels, "Transforming the Federal Emergency Management Agency: The Renewal and Revitalization of FEMA," in Mark A. Abramson and Paul R. Lawrence, eds., *Transforming Organizations*, Rowman and Littlefield Publishers, 2001; Patrick S. Roberts, "FEMA and the Prospects for Reputation-Based Autonomy," *Studies in American Political Development*, Vol. 20, No. 1, 2006.

Witt Ushered in Major Changes

One of Witt's signature initiatives focused on mitigation.[2] The mitigation grant program Project Impact was Witt's "first priority," according to Kay Goss, then–associate director for preparedness, training, and exercises, in 1998.[3] In his memoir, Witt explained that, for too long, EM focused on response after an event, and Witt wanted the field to become more proactive.[4]

Former EMI trainers and senior officials reported that courses focused on mitigation received more funding and attention during the Witt era: "Mitigation was the cornerstone of FEMA" during the period, and EMI reflected that focus and shifted further away from CD, according to two former trainers.[5]

Witt himself was a presence on campus. One EMI official from the Witt era reported seeing Witt sit in on classes in Emmitsburg while serving as FEMA administrator.[6] Witt was likely familiar with EMI in his prior role in state and local EM. FEMA administrators with SLTT EM experience are likelier than those without such experience to be familiar with EMI's work. (EMI staff reported seeing FEMA administrator Brock Long on campus regularly, too.[7] Long served as FEMA administrator from 2017 to 2019 and, like Witt, had served as a state-level emergency manager.)

One EMI trainer during the period described the Witt era as "Camelot" because EMI was held in high regard within FEMA, which reached a high point in its reputation. EMI was developing new courses "left and right," and it did not yet have to work through multiple organizational layers of FEMA or DHS as a whole. The period stands out in sharp relief against the changes that would follow the creation of DHS in 2002.[8] At the time, the superintendent reported to senior levels of FEMA.

Organizationally, Witt prioritized mitigation and all-hazards programs and deemphasized CD and national security. On September 7, 1993, Witt sent a memo to FEMA staff summarizing changes intended to achieve a "consolidation of functions, centralized management and administrative systems, and all-hazards operational capability, and equitable distribution of resources."[9] This included a reorganization that gave USFA oversight over the NETC campus, which included EMI.[10] Prior to this time, FEMA leadership, rather than USFA, which was one level down in the FEMA organization chart, had overseen the NETC campus. The combined shift in organization and change in emphasis on programs led the president of the American Federation of Government Employees' local union to outline how Witt's reorganization imposed significant costs on NETC and EMI and constrained their growth.[11] Although Witt is associated with a turnaround of

---

2 Phillips, Neal, and Webb, 2012, pp. 13, 328.

3 Preparedness Training and Exercises Directorate, FEMA, "Accomplishment of the Past, Visions of the Future," June 1998.

4 James Lee Witt and James Morgan, *Stronger in the Broken Places: Nine Lessons for Turning Crisis into Triumph*, Times Books, 2002, pp. 4–7.

5 Former senior EMI official, interview 2 with the author, December 13, 2021; former senior EMI official, interview 3 with the author, December 13, 2021.

6 Former senior EMI official, interview 3 with the author, December 13, 2021.

7 Former senior EMI official, interview 3 with the author, December 13, 2021.

8 Sharro, 2021.

9 "Witt Reinvents FEMA," 1993, p. 3.

10 "Witt Reinvents FEMA," 1993, p. 3.

11 John N. Peabody, Jr., president, American Federation of Government Employees Local 1983, prepared statement for U.S. Senate Hearing 105-427 on U.S. House of Representatives Bill 2158 and U.S. Senate Bill 1034 on appropriations for the U.S. Department of Veterans Affairs, the U.S. Department of Housing and Urban Development, and independent agencies for FY 1998, February 25, 1997.

FEMA, the period was more tumultuous for EMI. It lost focus on CD and national security, but it added programs to train FEMA staff.

The Emergency Management Institute Added a Mission: Training the Disaster Workforce

EMI added to its mission when it began training the FEMA disaster workforce. After an earthquake in Northridge, California, in 1994, EMI personnel provided on-the-spot training in response and recovery for local officials and FEMA personnel.[12] This was the first time that a field office had established a training component staffed with EMI personnel. In 1994, FEMA's Response and Recovery Directorate formally requested that EMI manage the training for FEMA's disaster workforce.[13] In 1996, EMI began formal programs to train FEMA staff in response and recovery, and, "by 2001, half of our work was dedicated to training FEMA staff," according to former EMI superintendent Sharro.[14] Prior to training the disaster workforce, EMI had not been able to take on new staff, but a senior EMI official from the period said that the Disaster Relief Fund "doubled our funding overnight."

The change in EMI followed the broader reorganization of the Witt era. Sharro explained that, after the Loma Prieta earthquake (1989) and Hurricanes Hugo (1989) and Andrew (1992), FEMA was judged to have not met expectations. After the Witt-era reorganization, "we had really changed the focus of this organization from looking exclusively outward to looking half outward, half inward." The main focus on looking inward was training FEMA staff to respond to and recover from disasters.[15]

Virtual Education Emerged as a Viable Option

At the same time that EMI and NETC reorganized internally, the world was becoming more digital. EMI had always offered distance learning by mail, but the 1980s brought new possibilities with video cassette recorders and then computer technology in offices and households.[16] EMI instructed a million people in distance learning per year by the late 1980s.[17] This could include everything from completing a course to viewing a videocassette.[18]

Distance learning included EMI self-study courses that reached people who could not attend classes in person in Emmitsburg, and it served as a bridge to EM for people in other professions, such as fire services or the military. Students would often use courses to earn points toward the CEM credential. Sometimes colleges and universities would require an EMI course as part of an EM-related degree or certificate program. The digital world added new means of completing these self-study courses, which were viral for growing the profession.

---

12 Lee Ireland, *The NFA-EMI Story*, Booksurge, 2008, p. 8; Sharro, 1995.

13 EMI, "Emergency Management Institute (EMI) Overview," webpage, last modified October 16, 2019c, p. 6.

14 Vogel and Gibbon, 2011.

15 Vogel and Gibbon, 2011.

16 Sharro, 1995.

17 Vogel and Gibbon, 2011.

18 Sharro, 1995.

In April 1988, the first Emergency Education Network broadcast was made from EMI.[19] This program was described as the "flagship of EMI's distance learning program."[20] It began in 1981 and offered free training and education to the public safety community (e.g., police, fire, and emergency responders) and the general public, with audiences in the hundreds of thousands in the 1980s. The live broadcasts covered such topics as hurricane preparedness, risk assessment, managing donations and volunteers, and search and rescue. The course topics were proposed by FEMA staff or requested by local groups that had particular needs. In some cases, the course design was modeled on college and university courses.[21] Many of the video broadcasts were interactive, and viewers could call in to the live broadcast. By the late 1990s, EMI was piloting programs to make the videos available via the internet as needed, rather than as live broadcasts. By 2003, NETC developed a virtual campus and was integrating approximately 40 independent study courses into the campus offerings.[22]

The Number of Higher Education Programs Grew

One of the biggest changes in EMI's relationship to the larger training and education ecosystem was the growth in EM higher education programs. EMI played a key role in fostering and coordinating the growth, beginning in the Witt era.

In the early 1990s, EMI convened a board of visitors chaired by Dennis S. Mileti, then a professor of sociology and natural-hazard researcher at Colorado State University (later and until his death in 2021, at the University of Colorado). In 1993, EMI held a higher education planning meeting that included Mileti and approximately a dozen professors. The group decided to hold an annual conference devoted to advancing college-level EM programs and to create instructor guides along with syllabi to disseminate knowledge.[23]

Two key leaders supported the development of the Higher Education Program and EMI's link to colleges and universities. Goss served as FEMA associate director (in charge of the Preparedness, Training, and Exercises Directorate) from 1994 to 2001. John McKay served as EMI superintendent from 1993 to 2000. Both recognized that there was a demand for more training than EMI could provide on its Emmitsburg campus. Distance education courses and training with state and local governments helped meet some demand, but Goss and McKay saw that higher education institutions would be natural partners to deliver training and education and to help build the profession of EM.[24]

In 1995, Goss selected Wayne Blanchard to lead the new Higher Education Program, working with college and university professors and other EM instructors to increase the use of EMI-developed courses and mate-

[19] USFA, 1999, p. 14.

[20] Carole Eiben and Bruce Marshall, "EENET: Emergency Education NETwork," edited version of July 8, 1998, online presentation for Emergency Information Infrastructure Partnership, circa 1998.

[21] Dennis Hickethier, Sue Mettlen, and Richard Muth, "Experiences with Distance Learning via the Internet," Emergency Information Infrastructure Partnership Virtual Library online presentation, January 14, 1998.

[22] Dennis Hickethier, "The Virtual Campus for the National Emergency Training Center (NETC)," Emergency Information Infrastructure Partnership Virtual Forum presentation, April 2, 2003.

[23] Thomas E. Drabek, *Social Problems Perspectives, Disaster Research and Emergency Management: Intellectual Contexts, Theoretical Extensions, and Policy Implications*, revision and expansion of the E. L. Quarantelli Award Lecture, EMI, August 2007b, p. 3; William L. Waugh, Jr., "Local Emergency Management in the Post-9/11 World," in William L. Waugh, Jr., and Kathleen J. Tierney, eds., *Emergency Management: Principles and Practice for Local Government*, 2nd ed., International City Management Association Press, 2007.

[24] Senior EMI official, interview 5 with the author, December 17, 2021; Waugh and Goss, 2019.

rials.[25] Blanchard had worked in CD programs, but he had a Ph.D. in history and had written on the history of CD. Goss saw in him an ability to see the bigger picture of a changing EM profession, growing beyond its CD past.[26]

Blanchard thrived in the role (as attested to by the creation of an award for EM education excellence in his name).[27] He sent out weekly emails, news items, think pieces, and scholarly articles and recommended course syllabi and books for graduate students.[28] EMI assembled a compilation of 70 college syllabi, with instructors' guides, and circulated the package as a way to seed knowledge about EM. At the time, colleges offered scattered courses on natural hazards, primarily in sociology and engineering departments.

The first two fully developed courses to emerge from the higher education project were "Sociology of Disaster" and the "Social Dimensions of Disaster," reflecting sociologists' importance to the hazard field. By 1998, there were nine associate's degree programs in EM and five baccalaureate programs.[29]

The higher education project used individual courses to help build the field. Blanchard said in 2006 that "the need is for four-year emergency management degree programs."[30] Blanchard wrote that the "day is coming" when a mayor or city manager would hire an EM degree holder as emergency manager. Blanchard's vision was not merely a prediction: EMI's efforts helped expand higher education offerings and link EM degrees to the evolving field of practice through regular communication and an annual conference of instructors.[31] One of his goals was to develop an EM degree in every state.[32]

EMI's efforts to grow higher education programs in EM were helped by events that generated in interest the field. The terrorist attacks of September 11, 2001, and Hurricane Katrina in 2005 drew attention to the important role played by emergency managers and first responders to crises.[33] Entrepreneurial professors seemed drawn to the field, and universities likely invested because they saw opportunity.[34]

By 2007, there were more than 100 EM programs. When Blanchard retired in 2020, FEMA's college list of EM associate's, bachelor's, master's, and doctoral degree programs numbered more than 200, depending on

---

25 Thomas E. Drabek, "Emergency Management and Homeland Security Curricula: Contexts, Cultures, and Constraints," *Journal of Emergency Management*, Vol. 5, No. 5, 2007a; Drabek, 2007b; Waugh and Goss, 2019.

26 Senior EMI official, interview 5 with the author, December 17, 2021; former senior EMI official, interview 3 with the author, December 13, 2021; Waugh and Goss, 2019.

27 North Dakota State University, "Dr. B. Wayne Blanchard Award for Academic Excellence in Emergency Management Higher Education," webpage, last updated June 2, 2022.

28 Subcommittee on Emergency Communications, Preparedness, and Response; Committee on Homeland Security; U.S. House of Representatives, *Moving Beyond the First Five Years: Ensuring FEMA's Ability to Respond and Recover in the Wake of a National Catastrophe*, hearing, 110th Cong., 2nd Sess., April 9, 2008; Mike Walker, deputy director, FEMA, statement for the record before the Subcommittee on Government Management, Information, and Technology; Committee on Government Reform; U.S. House of Representatives hearing titled "Year 2000 Emergency Management," 106th Cong., 1st Sess., March 22, 1999, p. 76; Waugh and Goss, 2019.

29 Preparedness, Training, and Exercises Directorate, 1998, p. 2.

30 Wayne Blanchard, "FEMA Emergency Management Higher Education Project Update," remarks made at the Emergency Management and Homeland Security/Defense Higher Education Conference, June 2006.

31 Blanchard, 2006.

32 Waugh and Goss, 2019.

33 Drabek, 2007a; Kathleen J. Tierney, "Testimony on Needed Emergency Management Reforms," *Journal of Homeland Security and Emergency Management*, Vol. 4, No. 3, 2007.

34 Major crises or focusing events can shift professors' teaching and research interests. For one example, see University of South Carolina professors' reflections on the impact of the September 11, 2001, attacks (Office of Communications and Public Affairs, University of South Carolina, "Scholarship, Research, and the Legacy of 9/11," webpage, updated September 9, 2021).

what variety of program was counted.[35] By then, he had supervised the development of 22 college courses, many of which were posted on EMI's website and adopted for use as is or modified by college and university instructors.[36]

The development of the Higher Education Program is regarded as a successful innovation, but the EMI of that period faced fewer layers of approval for new programs, and fewer other educational and training institutions offering similar courses. The FEMA headquarters of the late 1990s was smaller than it would be two decades later, and there was neither a DHS nor any homeland security educational programs separate from EM. One former senior EMI official wondered whether the "management by walking around" style of McKay and the relationships that drove the creation of the Higher Education Program would be possible decades later in a more complex organizational environment.[37]

Figure 5.1 shows the growth in EM programs over time, spawned by the Higher Education Program (renamed from "Higher Education Project" in 2008). After reaching more than 150 programs in 2007, the number stagnated until 2016, according to available data. After 2016, investments in program leadership and new partnerships led to a more than doubling of the number of programs. The Higher Education Program was moved from EMI to FEMA's National Training and Education Division in 2017, but it continued to use the NETC campus in Emmitsburg for conferences, and many EMI courses and materials are used by instructors in higher education.

FIGURE 5.1

Number of Emergency Management Undergraduate, Graduate, and Certificate Programs, 1983–2022

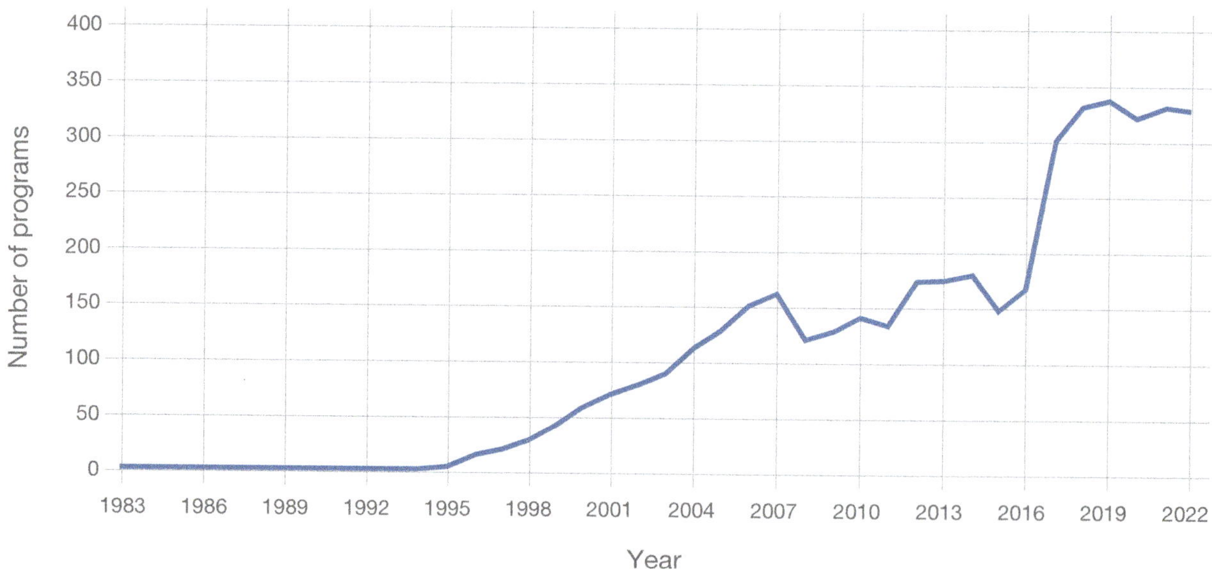

SOURCE: Adapted from Blanchard, 2008. The full source list is provided in the appendix.

[35] FEMA, "Higher Education Program," webpage, last updated June 14, 2022e.

[36] Comfort, Waugh, and Cigler, 2012; Waugh and Goss, 2019.

[37] Former senior EMI official, interview 3 with the author, December 13, 2021.

New Investments Were Made in Train-the-Trainer Approaches

The Witt era also brought new approaches to education and training. EMI reinvested in the train-the-trainer approach: Train people who would offer training throughout the country to people who might not attend EMI courses on their own as a way to expand EMI's reach and impact.[38] EMI and CDSC had always leveraged their limited resources this way, but, during the Witt era, EMI expanded train-the-trainer programs to new topics and invested in developing procedures for how to train trainers. In 1998, for example, EMI created new master trainer courses, including courses in mitigation, in terrorism consequence management, and for specific groups, such as attorneys general.[39]

The Emergency Management Institute Had an International Impact After the Cold War

Although EMI's primary audience was American, its courses and approach to exercises attracted attention around the world. Goss described a growing international presence in the late 1990s. "Our work is going global," Goss wrote in a FEMA document. "The international interest in our emergency preparedness and management programs has grown at a fantastic rate, due in large part to the information age technologies of CNN and e-mail."[40] For example, the Republic of Ireland adopted EMI courses in how to fight floods.[41]

Much of EMI's international involvement was support for programs at the end of the Cold War after the breakup of the USSR in 1991. Goss led a partnership with Russia's equivalent to FEMA (the Ministry of Emergency Situations), a delegation to the North Atlantic Treaty Organization, and an exercise in Iceland in 1998, drawing on much of the knowledge developed at and through EMI.[42]

One of the largest and most-successful programs at the end of the Cold War was the U.S.–Russian Cooperative Threat Reduction Program, also known as the Nunn–Lugar Cooperative Threat Reduction Program after two of its sponsors, Senators Sam Nunn and Richard Lugar. The program assisted Russia, Ukraine, Belarus, and Kazakhstan with consolidating nuclear weapons and removing fissile material after the breakup of the USSR. The project, which lasted from 1992 to 2012, was all the more remarkable because of Cold War tensions, and it reduced the spread of nuclear weapons and prevented them from spreading to new states and nuclear material from falling into the hands of criminal or terrorist organizations.

EMI's small role in the larger effort was to provide training for state and local officials on nuclear attack preparedness, including missiles and smaller "dirty bombs" set off in particular locations, as well as other chemical and biological threats (i.e., weapons of mass destruction, or WMDs). The Nunn–Lugar program devoted funds to support training state and local authorities because of a perceived gap in understanding about the WMD threat and what to do about it.[43] For example, in 1997, Nunn–Lugar funds supported EMI

---

[38] Subcommittee on National Security, Veterans Affairs, and International Relations; Committee on Government Reform; U.S. House of Representatives, *Combating Terrorism: Proposed Transfer of the Domestic Preparedness Program*, 106th Cong., 1st Sess., May 26, 1999.

[39] Preparedness, Training, and Exercises Directorate, 1998, p. 2.

[40] Preparedness, Training, and Exercises Directorate, 1998, p. 4.

[41] Preparedness, Training, and Exercises Directorate, 1998, p. 2.

[42] Kay C. Goss, visiting professor of political science, executive in residence, and interim director for international studies, University of Arkansas, biography, undated; Preparedness, Training, and Exercises Directorate, 1998, p. iv.

[43] William J. Clinton, "Report on Government Capabilities to Respond to Terrorist Incidents Involving Weapons of Mass Destruction: Message from the President of the United States," *Congressional Record*, Vol. 143, No. 22, February 26, 1997, p. H657.

training programs conducted jointly with DoD to prepare Anchorage and Seattle for terrorist attacks.[44] FEMA/EMI also worked with partner agencies to provide training. For example, EMI worked with the U.S. Army to prepare communities located near Army chemical stockpiles to protect themselves in case of an accident.[45] EMI partnered with DoD to provide senior officials training to prepare for the WMD threat.[46]

The Emergency Management Field Recognized Gender Diversity Issues

Although the institutional logic of EMI shifted during the late 1990s from its CD paramilitary past toward all-hazards EM,[47] the EM workforce remained largely unchanged. In particular, most managers were still men. Research shows that formal education and professionalization can help incorporate more women into historically male fields.[48] EMI training provided one potential route into the profession for women seeking to demonstrate their competence and preparation rather than relying on personal networks for hiring.[49]

Women were in "short supply," according to a 1999 survey of gender in the profession.[50] Some longtime emergency managers got their start in CD, and many newcomers entered the profession after serving in the military, fire, or police services. Scholars considered EM a gendered profession, meaning that it was a male domain.[51] When people talk about a profession using language associated with male or female traits, they can create social structures and a taken-for-grantedness that defines the job as male. For example, language of "mounting an aggressive, full-force response" to a disaster might come across as male, while language about "helping people and families" after a flood might come across as more female. Neither of these phrases is bad in and of itself, but scholars found that the cumulative effect of language and practices in the EM of the time made it perceived as a male environment in a way that was taken for granted and seen as natural.[52]

There was a small number of women in the 1980s—one small study of local EM directors identified only one woman.[53] By the 1990s, the number of women appears to have grown. Researchers on a 1998 study in Florida found that 15 percent of county office of EM directors and 13.5 percent of assistant directors were women.[54]

---

44 Preparedness, Training, and Exercises Directorate, 1998.

45 Chemical Stockpile Emergency Preparedness Program, homepage, undated; Clinton, 1997, p. H657.

46 Subcommittee on National Security, Veterans Affairs, and International Relations, 1999, p. 46; Office of Justice Programs, U.S. Department of Justice, "Nunn-Lugar-Domenici Domestic Preparedness Program: Program Overview," fact sheet, September 2001.

47 Russel R. Dynes, "Problems in Emergency Planning," *Energy*, Vol. 8, No. 8–9, August–September 1983.

48 Caroline Berggren and Nathanael Lauster, "The Motherhood Penalty and the Professional Credential: Inequality in Career Development for Those with Professional Degrees," *International Studies in Sociology of Education*, Vol. 24, No. 1, 2014; Rosemary Crompton and Kay Sanderson, "Credentials and Careers: Some Implications of the Increase in Professional Qualifications Amongst Women," *Sociology*, Vol. 20, No. 1, February 1986.

49 Jennifer Wilson, "Professionalization and Gender in Local Emergency Management," *International Journal of Mass Emergencies and Disasters*, Vol. 17, No. 1, March 1999.

50 Wilson, 1999.

51 Judith Lorber, "The Social Construction of Gender," in Estelle Disch, ed., *Reconstructing Gender: A Multicultural Anthology*, McGraw-Hill Higher Education, 1994; Wilson, 1999.

52 Lorber, 1994; Wilson, 1999.

53 Drabek, 1987.

54 Wilson, 1999.

The Institute of Emergency Administration and Planning at the University of North Texas offered one of the first EM degree programs. During its early years, from 1985 to 1989, its director reported that women made up approximately 20 percent of students. The number rose to 40 percent in 1998.[55] The pattern in the United States appears to be repeated elsewhere. There is no single study of women in the period that surveyed all emergency managers, so state-focused or convenience sample studies provide the best data available.

At the same time as women were slowly becoming more incorporated into the profession, the social science study of disasters focused more on gender.[56] Scholars posed questions about the gendered nature of the profession, how more women could be incorporated, and what value they might provide. One conclusion from this work was that more women could be incorporated into the field through training and education.[57]

EM also lacked representation of racial and ethnic minorities, although frank discussions in EM agencies and Congress appeared more common in 2020 than in 2000.[58] During the early 2000s, research focused on the ways in which disasters had disproportionate impacts on historically marginalized communities. In 2006, Hurricane Katrina showed how longstanding policies increased the vulnerability of the neighborhoods in which Black Americans lived.[59] Research during the first decade of the 2000s on the disproportionate impacts of disasters and social equity laid the foundation for later training courses on improving equitable outcomes and creating equity standards for recovery.[60]

The Field Is Growing and Diversifying—but Progress Is Slow

In 2022, FEMA administrator Deanne Criswell stressed the importance of diversifying the EM workforce at a hearing of the U.S. House of Representatives' Committee on Homeland Security Subcommittee on Emergency Preparedness, Response and Recovery:[61]

> We also know the more our workforce resembles the nation we serve, the better that we will serve it, [she said.] We are adapting our recruiting efforts to reach individuals from underrepresented communities by partnering with organizations like historically black colleges and universities and other minority-serving institutions.

Diversifying the workforce is also part of the FY 2022–2026 FEMA strategic plan.[62] Research shows that diverse teams can perform better by bringing different perspectives to the table. This might be especially

---

55 Wilson, 1999, p. 115.

56 Elaine Enarson and Betty Hearn Morrow, *The Gendered Terrain of Disaster: Through Women's Eyes*, Praeger, 1998; David M. Neal and Brenda Phillips, "Female-Dominated Local Social Movement Organizations in Disaster-Threat Situations," in Guida West and Rhoda Lois Blumberg, eds., *Women and Social Protest*, Oxford University Press, 1990; Brenda Phillips, "Gender as a Variable in Emergency Response," in Robert C. Bolin, ed., *The Loma Prieta Earthquake: Studies of Short-Term Impacts*, Institute of Behavioral Science, University of Colorado, 1990.

57 Wilson, 1999.

58 Thomas Frank, "Disaster Management Is Too White, Official Tells Congress," *Scientific American E&E News*, July 29, 2020.

59 Susan L. Cutter, Christopher T. Emrich, Jerry T. Mitchell, Bryan J. Boruff, Melanie Gall, Mathew C. Schmidtlein, Christopher G. Burton, and Ginni Melton, "The Long Road Home: Race, Class, and Recovery from Hurricane Katrina," *Environment: Science and Policy for Sustainable Development*, Vol. 48, No. 2, 2006; Camilla Stivers, "'So Poor and So Black': Hurricane Katrina, Public Administration, and the Issue of Race," *Public Administration Review*, Vol. 67, December 2007.

60 Melissa L. Finucane, Linnea Warren May, and Joan Chang, *A Scoping Literature Review on Indicators and Metrics for Assessing Racial Equity in Disaster Preparation, Response, and Recovery*, RAND Corporation, RR-A1083-1, 2021.

61 Bridget Johnson, "'Unrelenting' Disasters Compel FEMA to Take 'Deep Dive' into Assessing Future Workforce, Criswell Says," *Government Technology and Services Coalition Homeland Security Today*, June 16, 2022.

62 FEMA, 2021d.

true in disaster preparedness contexts, in which it is important to reach many different kinds of communities with different languages and cultures. Although the FEMA administrator's comments were about the FEMA organization, diversity and inclusion remain an issue for EM writ large.

Over time, the field has slowly diversified in terms of the racial, ethnic, gender, and professional backgrounds of its members.[63] However, as of 2019, it was still a predominantly white and male field, with two male EM directors for every female one, according to census and American Community Survey data.[64]

Research into how to incorporate underrepresented groups into the profession has shown that some strategies can improve pipelines into the profession and retention of underrepresented groups. These strategies include formal and informal mentorship, opportunities to build professional networks, continuing education, and formal credentials.[65]

EMI has contributed to diversifying the profession over time. EMI's on-site programs offer opportunities to build networks and form mentoring relationships. They also offer formal training and the opportunity to build credentials to allow new entrants into the profession. Diversity includes ability and disability in addition to race, ethnicity, and gender. For example, EMI has helped FEMA's Office of Disability Integration and Coordination develop educational content for people with disabilities.[66]

EMI itself has struggled with increasing the racial and ethnic diversity of its staff, even though many of its leaders have made diversity a priority. One senior official admitted that "the biggest single failure . . . during my time there was that we were unable to create a staff that had the same diversity as our audience."[67] One reason given was that the Emmitsburg area was not racially and ethnically diverse. In the 2010 census, the town was 95-percent white.[68]

Nonprofit organizations dedicated to building recruitment pipelines to increase diversity and inclusion in EM emerged during the 2000s. In 2014, the William Averette Anderson Fund was created to expand the number of people from historically underrepresented groups working in hazard and disaster research and practice.[69] The group focused its efforts on mentoring graduate students in the field. In 2020, Chauncia Willis and Curtis Brown founded the Institute for Diversity and Inclusion in Emergency Management with a vision to "[empower] marginalized communities within all phases of the disaster cycle."[70] Their goals included cultivating EM leaders and increasing the number of women and people of color in the EM profession. In addition, EM professional associations have adopted diversity, equity, and inclusion strategies and programs.

---

[63] John Weaver, Lindsey C. Harkabus, Jeffry Braun, Steven Miller, Rob Cox, John Griffith, and Rebecca J. Mazur, "An Overview of a Demographic Study of United States Emergency Managers," *Bulletin of the American Meteorological Society*, Vol. 95, No. 2, 2014.

[64] Data USA, "Emergency Management Directors," webpage, undated.

[65] Brenda D. Phillips, David M. Neal, and Gary R. Webb, "The Next Generation of Emergency Managers and Disaster Scientists," in Brenda D. Phillips, David M. Neal, and Gary R. Webb, eds., *Introduction to Emergency Management and Disaster Science*, Routledge, 2021.

[66] U.S. Senate, "Amendments Proposed and Submitted," *Congressional Record*, Vol. 164, No. 96, June 11, 2018.

[67] Former senior EMI official, interview 5 with the author, December 17, 2021.

[68] Maryland Department of Planning, Projections and Data Analysis, "2010 Census Profile of General Population and Housing Characteristics," undated.

[69] William Averette Anderson Fund, "Mission," webpage, undated.

[70] Institute for Diversity and Inclusion in Emergency Management, "Our Goals," webpage, undated.

Demand for Education and Training Outpaced Budgets

The Witt era at FEMA ended with the agency's reputation rehabilitated. FEMA became an attractive brand name in government, and it drew increasing attention in the 24-hour news cycle that emerged during cable news and early internet communications of the 1990s. However, EMI itself suffered from a lack of resources. Training needs for the growing profession outpaced budgets. There were more emergency managers, and they needed new collaborative, policy, and planning skills beyond the paramilitary processes that grew out of CD, and they faced new threats, including WMDs and terrorism. The U.S. Congress took note, and a House conference noted that "FEMA may not have adequate resources available for the training of federal, state, local, and volunteer disaster officials on the latest techniques in disaster response and resource management."[71] The conference directed FEMA to study the merits of establishing a new training academy in Florida—either supplementing or even replacing EMI. Although EM had become more prominent, EMI itself faced a growing demand for its education and training services from states and localities.

---

[71] U.S. House of Representatives, "Conference Report on H.R. 2684, Departments of Veterans Affairs and Housing and Urban Development, and Independent Agencies Appropriations Act, 2000," *Congressional Record*, Vol. 145, No. 138, October 13, 1999, p. H10023.

CHAPTER 6

The Homeland Security Era, 2001–2020

Summary

During this period, EMI added a focus on homeland security, which included preparedness for and responses to the threats of terrorism and mass-casualty events. Two seminal events gave impetus to this change:

- the September 11, 2001, terrorist attacks and the subsequent creation of DHS, into which FEMA was folded
- Hurricane Katrina in 2005 and its extended aftermath.

EMI offered new courses on homeland security issues but did not substantially change its curriculum following the creation of DHS.

Following concerns about the federal response to Katrina, the federal government strengthened the EM profession, training systems, and career pathways.

The field of EM grew in scope and complexity. In response, EMI developed an innovative integrated EM course (IEMC) that offered a single approach to preparing for and responding to crises. The course has become a cornerstone of FEMA's current curriculum.

EM developed as a profession through a growth in the number of degree programs, credentials (e.g., CEM), and full-time positions. Homeland security's path to professionalization was more uncertain, however, because the field was newer and the body of knowledge less developed.

The terrorist attacks of September 11, 2001, refocused the United States on the emergencies for which it should prepare and led to the formation of DHS. On that date, 19 al Qaeda men hijacked four commercial airplanes and crashed three of them into buildings: two World Trade Center towers in New York and the Pentagon outside Washington, D.C. A third plane crashed in Shanksville, Pennsylvania, after passengers stormed the cockpit to prevent the plane from hitting its likely target in Washington, D.C. The images of these attacks and their consequences brought the possibilities of large-scale terrorist attacks to the forefront of the national agenda. In 2002, the government responded by creating DHS and new authorities contained in the Homeland Security Act to prepare for terrorism and attacks. The attacks also led to more homeland security–focused institutions and programs in the education and training ecosystem.

The Creation of the U.S. Department of Homeland Security and the Homeland Security Institutional Logic

The creation of a new department added a new organization and new ideas for EMI and the EM field. Organizationally, creation of DHS increased the number of organizational layers, political appointees, and processes through which FEMA and EMI had to work to accomplish their mission. FEMA no longer reported directly to the White House, and, in many cases, it worked with other federal agencies through DHS rather than directly. EMI had to work through additional layers as well, including the newly created DHS Preparedness Directorate, where most FEMA functions resided.

Some observers called the creation of DHS the largest government reorganization since the National Security Act of 1947 created DoD and the Central Intelligence Agency.[1] DHS is a large agency. It began with plans for 180,000 employees, but, by 2018, it had 240,000. EMI's full-time staff of 86 in 2018 was dwarfed by that of the large department.[2]

The creation of DHS also yielded a new institutional logic of homeland security. The logic was characterized by the DHS organizational structure that brought together border and immigration agencies with FEMA and by a focus on the threat of international terrorism. The homeland security logic contrasted with EM logic even though it incorporated EM's preparedness, response, and recovery phases and a concern for natural disasters, although in a secondary position behind terrorism and attack.

Homeland security was a nebulous concept. Before 2001, the term was used in DoD to refer to programs to protect against foreign attack, but, after 2001, it was repurposed to describe the security of the United States more broadly.[3] Analysts authoring a 2013 Congressional Research Service report found that, more than a decade after 2001, the government still did not have a single definition of *homeland security*.[4] Similarly, in a study of state-level definitions of homeland security, researchers found no consistent definition across state homeland security organizations.[5]

An influential article in *Homeland Security Affairs* identified seven plausible definitions for *homeland security*, but its author argued that no single consistent definition was necessary and that, in fact, many important concepts have multiple definitions.[6] The article identified the core of homeland security as a combination of three topics: terrorism, national security, and all hazards. Homeland security addressed these topics by analyzing the risk of various threats and hazards and then managing their consequences. A terrorist attack led to the creation of DHS, but the department and associated policies addressed more than just terrorism.

In national security circles, the term *homeland defense* was used to refer to DoD efforts to protect the boundaries of the United States. It involved the military, whereas *homeland security* was used to refer to nonmilitary functions. Homeland defense is related to national security, but the latter is a broader category that deals more with alliances and the projection of power abroad.[7] Homeland security, homeland defense, and national security are all related, but the military has a greater role in the latter two.

---

[1] David Heyman and James Jay Carafano, *Homeland Security 3.0: Building a National Enterprise to Keep America Safe, Free, and Prosperous*, Heritage Foundation Special Report, Center for Strategic and International Studies, SR-23, September 18, 2008, p. 3.

[2] EMI, *Fiscal Year 2019 Annual Report*, 2019b.

[3] Elizabeth Becker, "Washington Talk: Prickly Roots of Homeland Security," *New York Times*, August 31, 2002.

[4] Shawn Reese, *Defining Homeland Security: Analysis and Congressional Considerations*, Congressional Research Service, RL42462, version 6, January 8, 2013.

[5] Scott E. Robinson and Nicola Mallik, "Varieties of Homeland Security: An Assessment of US State-Level Definitions," *Journal of Homeland Security and Emergency Management*, Vol. 12, No. 1, 2015.

[6] Christopher Bellavita, "Changing Homeland Security: What Is Homeland Security?" *Homeland Security Affairs*, Vol. 4, June 2008.

[7] Randall J. Larsen and Ruth A. David, "Homeland Defense: Assumptions First, Strategy Second," *Homeland Security*, October 2000, p. 2.

The *Homeland Security Affairs* article incorporated all-hazards as a third part of homeland security. Using the term *all-hazards* helps ensure that homeland-focused programs do not address the terrorist threat to the exclusion of other dangers.

Homeland Security Affairs was created in 2005 and is published by the Naval Postgraduate School's Center for Homeland Defense and Security (CHDS), which receives funding from FEMA. It is only one journal, but its creation is a sign that, by 2008, a different logic had emerged, and that logic attempted to incorporate all-hazards EM. However, some of the criticism of the DHS response to natural disasters was that it focused on terrorism to the exclusion of other, likelier threats and hazards.

In 2010, DHS's chief strategy document, the Quadrennial Homeland Security Review (QHSR), described homeland security as the "intersection of evolving threats and hazards with traditional governmental and civic responsibilities for civil defense, emergency response, law enforcement, customs, border patrol, and immigration."[8] The 2014 review added the goals of risk analysis and greater involvement with stakeholders, including SLTTs.[9] The QHSR was issued only twice, and DHS moved toward more midlevel strategic documents and high-level goals. It might issue a QHSR in the future, but the lack of a regular review is a sign that the institutional logic of homeland security is still evolving.

For EMI, homeland security brought new priorities and new organizational routines that added to and sometimes distracted from the EM mission. In some cases, EMI simply expanded its all-hazards approach to include a renewed focus on international terrorism. In other cases, the nebulous concept of homeland security added other factors, and new homeland security–focused training and education programs and institutions emerged that only partially overlapped with EMI.

Figure 6.1 shows the relative frequency of mentions of the phases of mitigation, preparedness, response, and recovery in EMI annual reports as an indicator of attention to these phases more broadly. The figure also shows a new phase, prevention, which was more common in the homeland security era because *prevention* generally referred to preventing terrorist attacks. Prevention and preparedness are coded together because the meanings of the terms overlap, both referring to efforts before an event. *Mitigation*, in contrast, has a more specific meaning, referring to efforts to reduce the losses that will be caused by inevitable disasters and events.

EMI annual reports reflect an emphasis on mitigation relative to mentions of other phases from 1998 through 2002, following the Witt-era reorganization. In the homeland security era, mentions of mitigation almost disappear, according to available data. The shift might reflect the homeland security era's focus on preventing attack rather than mitigating natural hazards.

8 DHS, *Quadrennial Homeland Security Review Report: A Strategic Framework for a Secure Homeland*, February 2010, p. viii.

9 DHS, *The 2014 Quadrennial Homeland Security Review*, June 18, 2014.

FIGURE 6.1

Evolving Emphasis on the Phases of Emergency Management, 1979–2019

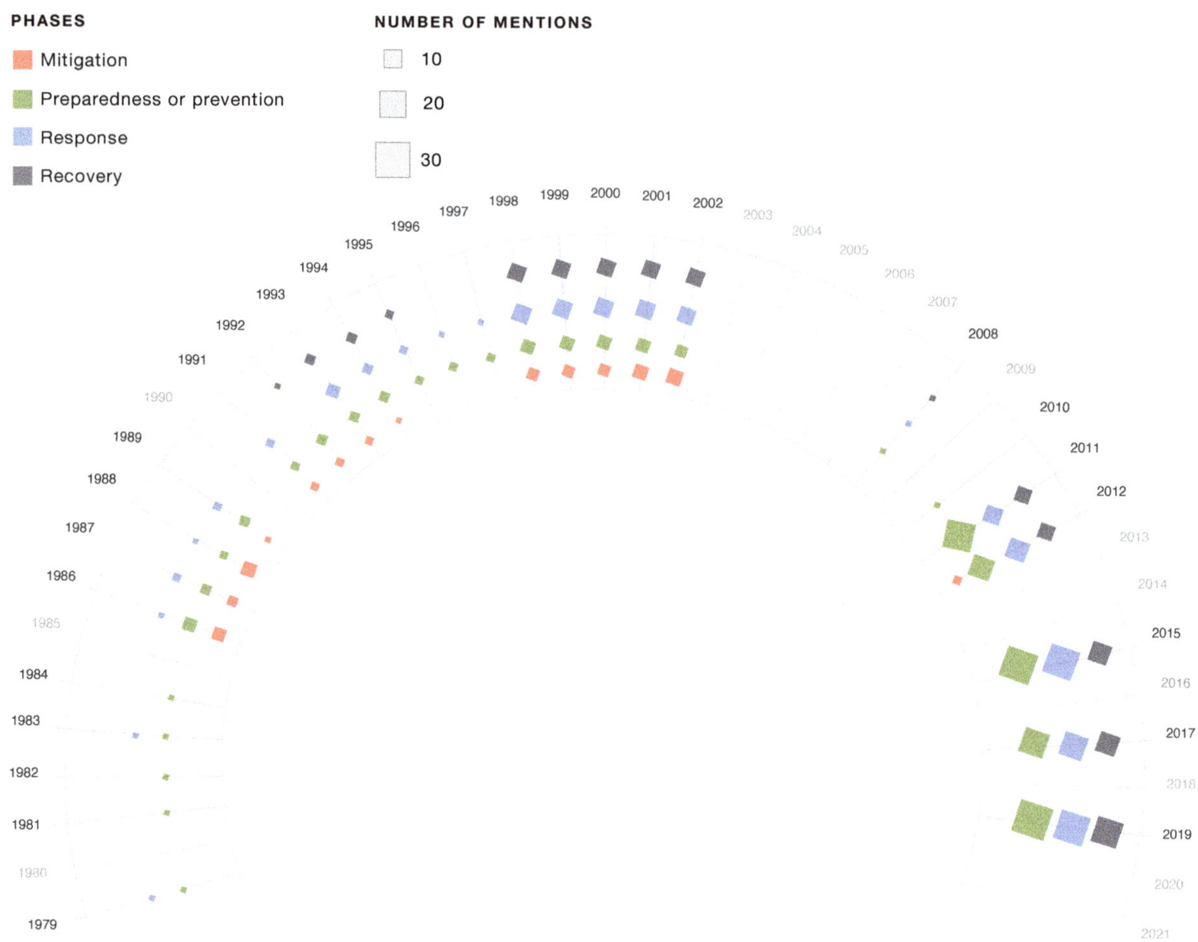

SOURCES: Features information from DCPA, 1972; DCPA, 1974; DCPA, 1975; DHS, 2013; DHS, 2015a; DHS, 2016; DHS, 2017; EMI, 1983; EMI, 1984; EMI, 1986; EMI, 1987; EMI, 1988; EMI, 1989; EMI, 1991; EMI, 1992; EMI, 1993; EMI, 1994; EMI, 1995; EMI, 1996; EMI, 1997; EMI, 1998; EMI, 1999; EMI, 2000; EMI, 2001; EMI, 2002; EMI, 2008; EMI, 2009; EMI, 2011; EMI, 2012a; EMI, 2012b; EMI, 2013; EMI, 2015; EMI, 2017; EMI, 2018; EMI, 2019aEMI, 2020; FCDA, 1952; FCDA, 1953; FCDA, 1954; FCDA, 1955; FCDA, 1956; FCDA, 1957; FCDA, 1958; FEMA, 2017; FEMA, 2018a; FEMA, 2019a; FEMA, 2020a; FEMA, 2021a; OCD, 1962; OCD, 1963; OCD, 1964; OCD, 1966; OCD, 1967; OCD, 1968; OCD, 1969; OCDM, 1959; OCDM, 1960. Mentions of each phase were counted in annual reports, and the boxes indicate the number of mentions relative to mentions of other phases in the same year.

NOTE: Faded years are those for which I have no data. See the appendix for an extended discussion of data sources for EMI budgets and courses. After FEMA's creation in 1979, the EM field began to coalesce around the idea that the field was linked through phases of activity: mitigation, preparedness, response, and recovery. All were common to multiple kinds of hazards. Expertise in these phases constituted the core of EM, and it allowed the field to claim expertise in an all-hazards approach, with an unlimited number of types of emergencies, because the core knowledge was not about the hazard or threat itself but about the phases of the disaster cycle.

This figure shows the number of mentions of terms associated with each phase in EMI annual reports and, for 1979 through 1984, EMI-relevant portions of FEMA annual reports. The numbers provide a high-level overview of changing emphases in EMI.

Recovery first appears as a phase in 1992, when the field began to grapple with what might be needed to support long-term recovery after a series of disasters that led to a reorganization at FEMA in 1993. After the creation of DHS in 2002, prevention was added as a phase in large part because terrorist attacks could be prevented. Mitigation is mentioned much less often after 2002. EMI offered courses in hazard mitigation, but this term was not used as often as the names of other phases.

The Emergency Management Institute Offered New Courses on Terrorism

EMI remained focused on EM, but it incorporated new courses on the terrorist threat. EM offices in states and localities took different approaches to adapting to homeland security, however. Some incorporated *homeland security* into their names; some took on more paramilitary structure or joined public safety departments, while others remained as free-standing EM entities. Colleges and universities saw renewed interest in courses on terrorism, and terrorism experts seemed to appear out of nowhere.[10] The Naval Postgraduate School created CHDS in 2003 to develop homeland security leaders, and ideas. The center works in close cooperation with (and has been funded by) FEMA's National Preparedness Directorate.[11] It also produces the journal *Homeland Security Affairs*.

Education and training institutions integrated homeland security concerns into EM during this period. International terrorism was at the top of the list of concerns, but the homeland security focus also included the idea that terrorists could use nuclear, chemical, or biological weapons and that communities should be prepared for these attacks. The public picture of the threat focused on terrorist groups, rather than nation-states, as the perpetrators. One challenge during the period was how to integrate homeland security concerns with EM in a strategic manner, rather than just changing the names of existing programs and courses.[12] Most organizations took the concepts of all-hazards and all-phases and expanded them to meet new threats of the homeland security era. However, not all threats received sufficient attention or funding.

For example, biological threats, including deliberately released agents and infectious diseases, received attention as part of the focus on WMDs. One week after the attacks of September 11, 2001, anonymous letters laced with anthrax arrived at post offices, media companies, and congressional offices. Over the course of several months, five people were killed and 22 people were infected. The attacks revealed gaps in U.S. biodefense and public health systems.[13]

EMI offered courses on bioterrorism during this period. Its comprehensive public health concerns course included material to "foster cooperation and heighten awareness to the issues surrounding bioterrorism."[14] On March 1, 2003, EMI grew its training programs with the Centers for Disease Control and Prevention to include integrated EM of counterterrorism; incident command system (ICS) training for SLTTs, including health departments; and health care–specific training and exercises.[15]

Another consequence of the September 11 attacks was a focus on national special security events, such as presidential inaugurations or the Super Bowl, which could provide large targets for terrorists. EMI conducted training programs for SLTTs to prepare for "national special security events" with a focus on how to prepare

---

[10] Melissa De Witte, "How Stanford Scholars Are Teaching the Next Generation About 9/11," *Stanford News*, September 8, 2021; Lisa Stampnitzky, *Disciplining Terror: How Experts Invented "Terrorism,"* Cambridge University Press, 2013.

[11] Center for Homeland Defense and Security, Naval Postgraduate School, "About CHDS," webpage, undated.

[12] Drabek, 2007a, p. 4; Drabek, 2007b.

[13] Lawrence O. Gostin and Jennifer B. Nuzzo, "Twenty Years After the Anthrax Terrorist Attacks of 2001: Lessons Learned and Unlearned for the COVID-19 Response," *JAMA Network Open*, Vol. 326, No. 20, 2021.

[14] Subcommittee on International Security, Proliferation, and Federal Services; Committee on Governmental Affairs; U.S. Senate, *FEMA's Role in Managing Bioterrorist Attacks and the Impact of Public Health Concerns on Bioterrorism Preparedness*, hearing, 107th Cong., 1st Sess., July 23, 2001, p. 7.

[15] Select Committee on Homeland Security, U.S. House of Representatives, *How Is America Safer? A Progress Report on the Department of Homeland Security*, hearing, 108th Cong., 1st Sess., May 20, 2003, and May 22, 2003a, pp. 16–17.

for these large gatherings. For officials charged with preparing for special events who were not familiar with EM, EMI provided an introduction to the field.[16]

One interviewee who had served as a senior official during that period recalled that the creation of DHS led to new courses but did not change the curriculum as much as it pulled staff in different directions.[17] Counterterrorism had been a part of EMI's curriculum from the beginning, when Giuffrida and Villella arrived at FEMA and EMI from CSTI. Terrorism preparedness instruction at EMI never completely disappeared, but it received new emphasis after the 1995 Tokyo subway sarin gas attack that killed 12 people and injured more than 5,000.[18] The September 11, 2001, attacks again renewed interest in terrorism.

Many EMI staff were given assignments elsewhere in DHS, leaving them part time at EMI. One person who had been a senior EMI leader during this period recalled that "a lot of our staff were pulled in different directions."[19] One example was the George W. Bush administration's Citizen Corps initiative. Citizen Corps was designed to involve the public in homeland security.[20] EMI provided experts on a half-time basis for EM training in programs. One such program was FEMA's Community Emergency Response Team (CERT), which trained individuals in emergency preparedness and basic response. These initiatives might have amplified FEMA's impact and improved disaster preparedness, but they also consumed EMI staff time and attention.

With a renewed focus on security in the wake of the September 11 attacks, the U.S. House Select Committee on Homeland Security asked whether DHS was returning to CD. The written response from DHS Secretary Tom Ridge provided a matter-of-fact answer: "We do not envision a return to the civil defense programs but intend to continue with the ongoing evolution of all-hazards preparedness."[21]

One of the major impacts of the homeland security era on EM was an emphasis on the ICS. This is a standardized approach to coordinate emergency response. The terrorist attacks of September 11 showed the importance of a standardized protocol that many agencies could use to communicate during a novel disaster. ICS is a concept used to improve communication among agencies within a community and to build communication among local, state, and federal authorities and, in some cases, nonprofits (specifically, voluntary organizations active in disaster) and the private sector. In 2003, Homeland Security Presidential Directive 5 instructed DHS to implement a standardized approach to incident management for all agencies involved in responding to events.[22] DHS developed NIMS, which incorporates ICS. DHS mandated that NIMS (and, by implication, ICS) be used to manage emergencies in order to receive some federal grants. Policy dictated the use of ICS, but EMI still had to teach communities how to use it.

"If we hadn't made the blood-and-guts effort after 9/11, communities would still have their own systems [which would not easily communicate]," said one interviewee who had been an EMI senior leader during this period. "The goal [of EMI leadership] was to institutionalize it to everybody other than the fire community—they would readily adopt it, but others (especially law enforcement) were resistant to it."[23] After 2001, EMI

[16] Eric Tolbert, director, Response Division, Federal Emergency Management Agency, U.S. Department of Homeland Security, statement for a hearing titled *Terror Attacks: Are We Prepared?* before the Committee on Health, Education, Labor, and Pensions, U.S. Senate, 108th Cong., 2nd Sess., July 22, 2004, p. 25.

[17] Senior EMI official, interview 5 with the author, December 17, 2021.

[18] Senior EMI official, interview 5 with the author, December 17, 2021.

[19] Senior EMI official, interview 5 with the author, December 17, 2021.

[20] White House, "Executive Summary," webpage, April 2002.

[21] Select Committee on Homeland Security, 2003a, p. 138.

[22] George W. Bush, "Management of Domestic Incidents," Homeland Security Presidential Directive 5, February 28, 2003.

[23] Senior EMI official, interview 5 with the author, December 17, 2021.

created new courses to spread ICS across the country, and these courses became less common only when ICS began to be adopted as a standard.[24]

ICS was useful for many kinds of events, not just terrorism. With so much attention to the threat of terrorism through bombs, airplanes, and other WMDs, many state and local jurisdictions used EM training courses to improve their preparedness, incident command, and decisionmaking structures to prepare for a variety of events, not just international terrorism. One emergency manager in a tribal community summed up the challenge:

> When I began working in this field, I had to clear up the misconceptions of what Emergency Management actually does. My Tribal Council had the perception and ideology that, "why would Bin Laden come after the Little Traverse Bay Bands of Odawa Indians?" There had to be an approach to convince and get the buy-in for supporting Emergency Management. We were not necessarily protecting from terrorists but we were saving our people from the next outbreak or epidemic.[25]

The tribal emergency manager developed plans to prepare emergency kits stocked with food, water, medicine, and personal protective equipment. She encouraged households to make evacuation plans and be prepared to shelter in place. She worked with infrastructure owners and operators to increase protection from natural hazards, as well as deliberate ones. Despite the shift toward homeland security at the national level, many local-level managers continued to work to build processes to prepare for many kinds of emergencies.

The Emergency Management Institute Developed an Integrated Emergency Management Course

The growth in the complexity of EM, including new counterterrorism-focused programs and new entities, such as nonprofits, interested in EM led EMI to develop the exercise-based IEMC in stages during the 1990s. Figure 6.2 shows one of the courses being conducted.

The goal of the course is to integrate perspectives from a single community in responding to a crisis. Some of the courses are community-specific. They might bring in roughly 70 leaders, including emergency managers, public works directors, and nonprofit leaders, to Emmitsburg for a week for a mix of classroom instruction and scenario-based experiences. The course brings together officials who might not have worked together before to focus on how to integrate response in their particular community in advance of a crisis. For many communities, the courses helped build networks outside formal organizational lines of communication and ultimately improve disaster planning and response. One example of the program's success is in FEMA's attribution of Minneapolis's swift response to a deadly eight-lane bridge collapse in 2007 to the two IEMC courses that responders had taken before the event.[26]

The course quickly became a centerpiece of EMI education, according to Sharro, superintendent from 1990 to 2006:[27] "Focusing on interoperability and unity of effort among the various community organizations—fire, police, public works, emergency medical services, emergency management, mayor, city council, and

[24] Former senior EMI official, interview 3 with the author, December 13, 2021.

[25] Susan Gasco, "Three Things to Protect: Our Past, Present, and Future," National Emergency Management Advanced Academy paper, August 2019, p. 2.

[26] FEMA, "IEMC: Community-Specific," webpage, last updated November 3, 2020c.

[27] Sharro, 2021.

FIGURE 6.2
Participants in the Las Vegas Integrated Emergency Management Course Receive a Situation Update

SOURCE: Reproduced from EMI, 2019a.

public affairs—the demand for IEMCs skyrocketed" during the 1990s, according to Sharro.[28] IEMC instructors were also in demand. After the bombing of the Alfred P. Murrah Federal Building in Oklahoma City, Oklahoma, in 1995, the Oklahoma City Fire Department asked EMI to send the instructors from a recent Oklahoma City–focused IEMC to support and mentor leaders during the city's response. The IEMC instructors arrived in Oklahoma the day after the bombing to help. In 2007, FEMA administrator R. David Paulison mentioned the course to a U.S. House committee as one of FEMA's most-important training initiatives.[29]

Post-Katrina Reforms Strengthened Emergency Management Career Paths

Hurricane Katrina devastated coastal Louisiana and Mississippi in 2005, causing damage and loss of life far beyond what most Americans thought possible.[30] The storm led to the failure of the levee systems in New

---

[28] Sharro, 2021.

[29] Committee on Oversight and Government Reform, U.S. House of Representatives, *FEMA Preparedness in 2007 and Beyond*, hearing, 110th Cong., 1st Sess., July 31, 2007, p. 83.

[30] Michael D. Barnes, Carl L. Hanson, Len M. B. Novilla, Aaron T. Meacham, Emily McIntyre, and Brittany C. Erickson, "Analysis of Media Agenda Setting During and After Hurricane Katrina: Implications for Emergency Preparedness, Disaster Response, and Disaster Policy," *American Journal of Public Health*, Vol. 98, No. 4, April 2008; Andy Horowitz, *Katrina: A History, 1915–2015*, Harvard University Press, 2020.

Orleans, estimated damage of $180 billion, and 1,833 deaths.[31] The storm's effect on policy was to refocus attention away from terrorism and onto natural hazards.

Hurricane Katrina was a low point for FEMA's reputation, and it led to a period of self-reflection for the EM field. A U.S. House committee found a "failure of initiative" during the storm. The executive summary of findings noted that "[o]fficials at all levels seemed to be waiting for the disaster that fit their plans, rather than planning and building scalable capacities to meet whatever Mother Nature threw at them."[32] Although FEMA's missteps made headlines, investigations found failures at all levels of government.

The poor response drew attention to the lack of EM experience among FEMA appointees, including FEMA administrator Michael Brown.[33] He resigned in 2005 amid criticism of his leadership and three days after being removed from his duties overseeing hurricane relief. Before arriving at FEMA as a political appointee in 2001, Brown served for a decade as a commissioner at the International Arabian Horse Association. Brown then served as legal counsel to FEMA administrator Joe Allbaugh, who was a friend from college, before becoming administrator in 2003.[34]

Many observers thought that the response to the storm proved that federal homeland security policy and organization had shifted too far in the direction of terrorism preparedness and away from preparing for and responding to large-scale natural disasters that overwhelmed states and localities.[35] As a result, President George W. Bush signed the Post-Katrina Emergency Management Reform Act in October 2006 to improve and integrate preparedness and response authorities.[36] The act provided new authority for response efforts and reorganized FEMA. It moved FEMA out of the DHS Preparedness Directorate and made the agency into its own entity within DHS.[37] EMI was one of the entities moved into FEMA, without the Preparedness Directorate layer and, in 2007, moved out of USFA's jurisdiction.[38]

The act also strengthened the EM profession by requiring that FEMA maintain a well-trained disaster workforce. That broad goal led to new initiatives and new funding for EMI and its partners. EMI restructured and enhanced its disaster operations and recovery training.[39] It developed programs to help emergency

---

31 National Centers for Environmental Information, National Oceanic and Atmospheric Administration, "Billion-Dollar Weather and Climate Disasters," webpage, undated.

32 Select Bipartisan Committee to Investigate the Preparation for and Response to Hurricane Katrina, U.S. House of Representatives, *A Failure of Initiative: Final Report of the Select Bipartisan Committee to Investigate the Preparation for and Response to Hurricane Katrina*, 109th Cong., 2nd Sess., Report 109-377, February 15, 2006, p. 2.

33 David E. Lewis, *The Politics of Presidential Appointments: Political Control and Bureaucratic Performance*, Princeton University Press, 2010.

34 Lynn Neary, "FEMA Director Michael Brown Resigns," National Public Radio, September 12, 2005.

35 Cooper and Block, 2007; Roberts, 2013.

36 Analyst in EM policy, 2011.

37 FEMA, "Disaster Authorities," webpage, last updated July 6, 2021b; Subcommittee on Emergency Communications, Preparedness, and Response; Committee on Homeland Security; U.S. House of Representatives, *PKEMRA Implementation: An Examination of FEMA's Preparedness and Response Mission*, hearing, 111th Cong., 1st Sess., March 17, 2009.

38 EMI was transferred out of USFA's jurisdiction as part of the Department of Homeland Security Appropriations Act, 2007 (Pub. L. 109-295, 2006) (Subcommittee on Technology and Innovation, 2007).

39 EMI, *Fiscal Year 2012 Training Catalog*, 2012a, p. 109.

managers track performance improvement.[40] It developed new training in FEMA information technology systems.[41]

The act also required FEMA to publish information on EM career paths and led to the creation of the National Preparedness System, which provided a structure for EMI training.[42] EMI contributed to many of the reforms related to training and education led by other entities. For example, EMI participated in creating a credentialing plan for the disaster-surge workforce.[43]

The Emergency Management Institute Evolved Emergency Management Ideas and Doctrine

At the level of doctrine, EMI's director participated in the revision of the National Response Plan and the development of the eventual National Response Framework. The Post-Katrina Emergency Management Reform Act required DHS to replace the National Response Plan with a new plan that addressed some of the shortfalls in coordinating government and nongovernmental responses to disasters.[44] Many state and local emergency managers said that the plan presumed federal coordination and support that the government was not prepared to provide.[45] A more realistic approach would be to plan for more state and local involvement, mutual support, and leadership. The National Response Framework made strides in that direction.

Changing federal plans was not enough, however. The field needed to change along with the plans. In 2007, a group of stakeholders met at EMI under the direction of Blanchard and superintendent Cortez Lawrence to develop a guide for the field. The principles of emergency management defined the field as "the managerial function charged with creating the framework within which communities reduce vulnerability to hazards and cope with disasters."[46] The principles put forth a vision of how the intergovernmental system would work in a mutually supportive, rather than top-down, manner. The principles were finalized, approved, and circulated by FEMA, IAEM, NEMA, and the National Fire Protection Association. EMI posted the principles in its classrooms, and, by 2022, the principles had been downloaded 10,000 times from ResearchGate.[47]

EMI worked on planning to replace the National Response Plan alongside the newly created National Integration Center (NIC), which was given responsibility for doctrine development and had some training responsibilities.[48] The establishment of NIC created another source of FEMA-level EM doctrine that poten-

---

[40] U.S. Government Accountability Office (GAO), *FEMA Disaster Workforce: Actions Needed to Address Deployment and Staff Development Challenges*, GAO-20-360, May 4, 2020, p. 54.

[41] William O. Jenkins, Jr., director, homeland security and justice issues, GAO, *Actions Taken to Implement the Post-Katrina Emergency Management Reform Act of 2006*, report for congressional requesters, GAO-09-59R, November 21, 2008, p. 83.

[42] W. Jenkins, 2008.

[43] Subcommittee on Emergency Communications, Preparedness, and Response, 2009, p. 26. EMI worked with the Disaster Reserve Workforce Division of DHS to develop credentialing plans for a disaster assistance workforce.

[44] Analyst in emergency management policy, *The National Response Framework: Overview and Possible Issues for Congress*, Congressional Research Service, RL34758, January 21, 2011; Subcommittee on Economic Development, Public Buildings, and Emergency Management; Committee on Transportation and Infrastructure; U.S. House of Representatives, *Readiness in the Post-Katrina and Post-9/11 World: An Examination of the New National Response Framework*, hearing, 110th Cong., 1st Sess., September 11, 2007b.

[45] Select Bipartisan Committee to Investigate the Preparation for and Response to Hurricane Katrina, 2006, pp. 131, 156; GAO, *Catastrophic Disasters: Enhanced Leadership, Capabilities, and Accountability Controls Will Improve Effectiveness of the Nation's Preparedness, Response, and Recovery System*, GAO 06-618, September 6, 2006.

[46] IAEM, 2007, p. 4.

[47] IAEM, 2007.

[48] Committee on Homeland Security, U.S. House of Representatives, *The Challenge of Protecting Mass Gatherings in a Post-9/11 World*, hearing, 110th Con., 2nd Sess., July 9, 2008, p. 76; John Ford, FEMA, presentation at All-Hazards Incident Management Team Symposium, December 2018.

tially competed with EMI. EM never had a doctrine development and promulgation process as formal as the military's. However, the federal government does issue official plans, definitions, and advice that together make up doctrine that emergency managers adapt to specific situations and programs. Creating NIC was one attempt to rationalize doctrine development.

EMI, however, had established itself as an important source of ideas in the profession and an important convener, particularly of SLTT officials who did not work for FEMA. Prior to Katrina, multiple entities worked with EMI to create policies and training that were new doctrine or that communicated plans and concepts to SLTT partners. For example, when DHS Assistant Secretary for Infrastructure Protection Robert B. Stephan wanted to build consensus among SLTTs around new NIMS and National Response Plan guidance, he looked to EMI to deliver the training.[49] Some of EMI's budget fluctuations can be explained by FEMA or DHS officials outside of EMI providing funding and requests for EMI to deliver training in a new initiative.

After the creation of NIC, IAEM supported EMI's continuing role in doctrine development. IAEM president Michael D. Selves told a U.S. House subcommittee that IAEM "would support the Emergency Management Institute as the primary Federal entity for the development of general emergency management education, training, and doctrine."[50] EMI has established itself as a source of ideas, education, and training and as and a link between FEMA and the broader profession.

Practically speaking, EMI served as an arbiter when doctrine was inconsistent or did not meet the needs of SLTT partners. "EMI became an effective clearinghouse for those matters [i.e., doctrinal disputes] because EMI had objectivity," said a senior official who worked at EMI during the 2000s.[51] "We didn't have a fish to fry if there were doctrinal squabbles among different parts of the agencies." EMI's doctrinal role was not formal, but it emerged through the course of its work.

The Education and Training Ecosystem Expanded

By the 2010s, the number of EM education and training providers had grown, along with the number of professionals. The number of colleges and universities with degree and certificate programs in EM grew into the hundreds, and many more offered homeland security education.[52] Other parts of the federal government, too, provided education and training programs that complemented and, in some cases, overlapped with EMI's. Among the most prominent were the Naval Postgraduate School's CHDS in Monterey, California. Created in 2003 to educate current and emerging leaders in the new field of homeland security, CHDS offers a master's degree and other training and education programs aimed at primarily in-career professionals.[53] Many of these programs are delivered in partnership (and with funding from) FEMA's National Preparedness Directorate. CHDS also leads the University and Agency Partnership Initiative, which shares homeland security curricula among member institutions and offers a summer institute for instructors and homeland

[49] Committee on Homeland Security and Governmental Affairs, U.S. Senate, *Hurricane Katrina: The Roles of U.S. Department of Homeland Security and Federal Emergency Management Agency Leadership*, hearing, 109th Cong., 2nd Sess., February 10, 2006.

[50] Committee on Homeland Security and Governmental Affairs, 2006.

[51] Senior EMI official, interview 5 with the author, December 17, 2021.

[52] Waugh and Goss, 2019, pp. 7–10.

[53] CHDS, undated.

security program leaders.[54] During the 2010s, the initiative shared resources with EMI's Higher Education Program, and many universities and instructors participated in both.

Within FEMA, CDP in Anniston, Alabama, offers what it calls *all-hazards training*, but its expertise is in chemical, biological, radiological, nuclear, and high-yield explosive hazards and events. CDP trains many of the same civilian emergency responders from SLTTs, the federal government, and nonprofits and the private sector who might attend EMI during their careers. CDP's Noble Training Facility is the only facility in the United States dedicated to training hospital professionals in disaster response tailored to the hospital environment. CDP was formally created in 1998, although individual programs and facilities date back much earlier. The U.S. Army Chemical School, for example, was at Fort McClellan, Alabama, from 1979 until 1998; when the Army base closed as part of a 1995 Base Closure and Realignment Commission recommendation, and it became CDP.

During the early to mid-2000s, EMI was given responsibility for the Noble mass-casualty training center, which later became part of CDP. EMI integrated mass-casualty training into its courses and developed new courses focused specifically on hospitals.[55] Over time, DHS and FEMA integrated Noble and the larger CDP into a broader menu of classes and functions.[56]

As of this writing in 2022, FEMA operates other training and education centers in addition to CDP and NFA, mentioned earlier. It funds two consortia that provide training:

- The National Domestic Preparedness Consortium provides training for chemical, biological, radiological, and explosive hazards.
- The Rural Domestic Preparedness Consortium focuses on homeland security training for rural emergency responders.

In addition, FEMA provides training for community organizations, individuals, and households:

- The Organizations Preparing for Emergency Needs training supports community-based organizations, such as food pantries and day cares, planning to sustain operations during an emergency.
- You Are the Help Until Help Arrives Training is provided online to help people save lives before other responders arrive.
- CERT training is often provided by states and localities, but FEMA provides training materials on DHS's Ready.gov website, and EMI provides an independent study course in CERT.

These training programs supplement training offered by EMI.[57] These programs are less structured than EMI programs, such as the academy series, which provides a framework for gaining EM skills through basic, advanced, and executive courses.[58] The programs mentioned above target particular groups, whereas EMI provides training to a variety of audiences. One audience EMI rarely trains is internal FEMA staff. As of this writing in 2022, FEMA operates separate programs for staff development.

---

[54] CHDS, 2016.

[55] Sharro, 2021.

[56] Select Committee on Homeland Security, U.S. House of Representatives, *Hearing on Response to Terrorism: How Is the Department of Homeland Security Improving Our Capabilities*, 108th Cong., 2nd Sess., June 19, 2003b; Subcommittee on Emergency Preparedness, Science, and Technology; Committee on Homeland Security; U.S. House of Representatives, *The Proposed Fiscal Year 2007 Budget: Enhancing Preparedness for First Responders*, hearing, 109th Cong., 2nd Sess., February 8, 2006, pp. 13, 47–48.

[57] FEMA, "Training and Education," website, last updated July 14, 2022f.

[58] FEMA, "Emergency Management Professional Program (EMPP)," webpage, last modified May 23, 2022b.

During the 2000s, centers for homeland security research and teaching emerged. EM has long had active university-based centers, such as the Natural Hazards Center in Boulder (created in 1976) and the Disaster Research Center in Newark, Delaware (created in 1963 and moved from Ohio State to Delaware in 1985).[59] These centers often approached EM through the academic lenses of sociology or engineering.

Homeland security was new. CHDS emerged as a leader, and CDP maintained specialized facilities and expertise for chemical, biological, radiological, nuclear, and high-yield explosive threats, leaving EMI as a leader in EM. The task for EMI would be to define EM amid a changing threat and hazard landscape.

The growth in the number of new homeland security–focused providers raised the potential for duplication of training opportunities across the federal government. For example, the U.S. Department of Justice took on some homeland security training of SLTT partners, which some EMI trainers saw as a zero-sum budgeting game between EMI and other training institutions.[60]

In 2006, Congressional Research Service analyst Shawn Reese testified to the U.S. House Committee on Homeland Security about potential duplication of homeland security training.[61] The committee discussed the possible consolidation of counterterrorism training into one agency. DHS never ordered a formal consolidation, but EMI did work to integrate its offerings with those of other providers. That meant assessing what courses EMI would offer and to whom, and what would be better left to others.

EMI conducted a lot of hands-on, practical training that other organizations were not doing, according to one of EMI's leaders during the late 1990s and 2000s.[62] Because EMI was so focused on training early- and midcareer managers, it might have neglected education for the senior levels. "If I were doing it today, I would've drawn everything I could from CHDS in terms of executive senior leadership training," one EMI leader said.[63]

Ultimately, EMI's niche remained EM. Some other institutions offered training in related fields, and some individual emergency managers sought training and education at multiple institutions. EMI retained the EM brand, and it framed its approach through the all-hazards, all-phases, and incident command approaches to EM.

The Emergency Management Institute Outreach Sought to Engage the "Whole Community" and Stakeholders

EMI had always included nonprofit leaders in the IEMC and other programs. Beginning in 2009, however, FEMA developed the concept of the "whole community" as a foundation for resilience.[64] The concept of whole community is premised on the idea that nonprofits, community groups, businesses, and residents—not just government planners—should be involved in disaster preparedness and response at a community

[59] Enrico L. Quarantelli, "The Early History of the Disaster Research Center," undated.

[60] Former senior EMI official, interview 3 with the author, December 13, 2021.

[61] Subcommittee on Emergency Preparedness, Science, and Technology and Subcommittee on Management, Integration, and Oversight; Committee on Homeland Security, U.S. House of Representatives, *The National Training Program: Is Anti-Terrorism Training for First Responders Efficient and Effective?* 109th Cong., 1st Sess., June 23, 2005, pp. 43–44.

[62] Senior EMI official, interview 5 with the author, December 17, 2021.

[63] Senior EMI official, interview 5 with the author, December 17, 2021.

[64] FEMA, *A Whole Community Approach to Emergency Management: Principles, Themes, and Pathways for Action*, FDOC 104-008-1, December 2011.

level. The whole-community concept emerged along with greater use of the concept of resilience in EM. *Resilience* refers to the idea that communities should build the capacity to bounce back quickly after disasters.[65]

In 2009, FEMA administrator Craig Fugate requested that EMI expand its training programs to include participants from the whole community.[66] EMI adopted the concept as part of its recruitment and training materials. For example, it included representatives from voluntary organizations and the private sector as part of the target audience for its executive academy, a strategic-level senior leader course.[67] In 2022, EMI's new Vanguard Executive Crisis Leaders Fellowship for senior EM leaders explicitly included representation from the private sector, nonprofit organizations, and universities in addition to government officials.[68] The Homeland Security Operational Analysis Center supported this effort.

One of the most-significant developments in expanding the whole community was the explicit addition of tribal nations. The Stafford Act does not mention tribal governments, and the omission created ambiguity about FEMA's relationship to the tribes. Conceptually, tribes might always have been part of the whole-community idea, but they were not explicitly mentioned in the Stafford Act. In 2013, the Sandy Recovery Improvement Act amended the Stafford Act to provide tribal governments the option to request a presidential emergency or major disaster declaration independent of a state, after Sandy or future events.[69] The following year, EMI developed a curriculum for tribal nations and delivered it on site to tribes, as well as at EMI in Emmitsburg.[70]

Emergency Management Institute Superintendents Come from Emergency Management and Fire Backgrounds

All EMI superintendents have had some EM experience broadly construed, but some trends emerge over time. Early EMI superintendents were less likely to have served in EM operational roles because the profession was new. EMI's first superintendent, Ralph Bledsoe, was a political advisor to President Reagan and had participated in policy discussions about EM. He went on to work on the White House Domestic Policy Council after leading EMI. As a group, the superintendents have a mix of EM, FEMA management, and adult education experience. They were often paired with deputy administrators with complementary skills.[71] Some superintendents (e.g., Lawrence) had primarily fire management experience, but most had served in senior roles in FEMA. Figure 6.3 shows that tenures are between two and seven years.

[65] Alexander Fekete, Gabriele Hufschmidt, and Sylvia Kruse, "Benefits and Challenges of Resilience and Vulnerability for Disaster Risk Management," *International Journal of Disaster Risk Science*, Vol. 5, No. 1, March 2014.

[66] EMI, 2019c, p. 6.

[67] FEMA, "The National Emergency Management Executive Academy," webpage, last modified May 23, 2022c.

[68] Vanguard Senior Executive Leadership Program, "After Action Report," June 27, 2022.

[69] FEMA, "Tribal Affairs," webpage, last updated September 8, 2022g. The Sandy Recovery Improvement Act is Public Law 113-2, Disaster Relief Appropriations, January 29, 2013, Division B.

[70] Committee on Indian Affairs, U.S. Senate, *Emergency Management in Indian Country: Improving FEMA's Federal–Tribal Relationship with Indian Tribes*, hearing, 115th Cong., 1st Sess., February 8, 2017.

[71] Senior EMI official from interview 5, follow-up email to the author, August 1, 2022.

FIGURE 6.3
Emergency Management Institute Superintendents and Their Tenures

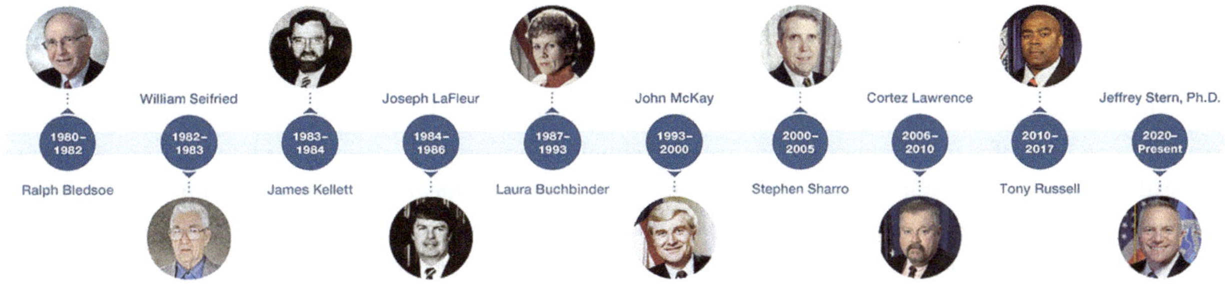

SOURCE: Features information from EMI, "List of Superintendents," 2022.

Civil Defense Offers a Legacy for Building National Resilience

By 2020, EMI and the broader field had multiple institutional logics on which to draw to meet their challenges. The logic of CD faded into the background, but it never completely disappeared even as the world changed since the Cold War. Russia's invasion of Ukraine in 2019 and threats from North Korea drew attention to the possibility of nuclear conflict and cyberattacks. COVID-19 showed the need to strengthen dormant processes for mobilizing national capabilities. *Mobilization* refers to processes to marshal national resources in the event of a disaster.[72] COVID-19 tested the United States' preparation for a truly national emergency in which there were simultaneous disaster declarations in all SLTTs, requiring a national-level mobilization at a level once envisioned in CD preparedness. Maintaining core social functions required skill in logistics and managing supply chains and the use of the Defense Production Act—all legacies of Cold War CD. As of 2022, EMI was deliberating about investments in these CD-legacy subjects.[73]

Maintaining national functions, including supply chains, health, transportation, and education, falls under the category of community lifelines.[74] FEMA formalized the concept of community lifelines in the 2019 edition of the National Response Framework.[75] The notion that identifying vulnerabilities in society's core functions and then protecting those functions is a core federal responsibility in managing emergencies has its roots in CD planning during the Cold War and even earlier in both world wars.[76]

Other legacies of CD are the notions that nation-state threats are among the national emergencies for which the United States must prepare and that all-hazards, all-phases emergency preparedness (or *dual use*, as it was once called) has benefits for multiple kinds of threats. After the fall of the Berlin Wall and the breakup of the USSR, nation-state threats receded from the national agenda. International terrorism drew

---

[72] Ting-An-Xu Liu, G. Breck Wightman, Euipyo Lee, and Jordan Hunter, "Revisiting 'Big Questions' of Public Administration After COVID-19: A Systematic Review," *Asia Pacific Journal of Public Administration*, Vol. 43, No. 3, 2021; Daniel Nohrstedt, "Explaining Mobilization and Performance of Collaborations in Routine Emergency Management," *Administration and Society*, Vol. 48, No. 2, March 2016; H. Daniel Xu and Rashmita Basu, "How the United States Flunked the COVID-19 Test: Some Observations and Several Lessons," *American Review of Public Administration*, Vol. 50, No. 6–7, August–October 2020.

[73] EMI staff members, communication to the author, April 12, 2022.

[74] FEMA, "Community Lifelines," webpage, last updated July 27, 2020b.

[75] FEMA, *National Response Framework*, 4th ed., October 28, 2019b.

[76] Collier and Lakoff, 2021.

more attention as a threat, as indicated by U.S. national security strategies and other formal documents.[77] The 2017 National Security Strategy returned focus to the threat posed by large states, not just terrorist groups, criminal networks, or global processes, such as climate change and migration.[78] Russia's 2022 invasion of Ukraine made the nation-state threat of territorial conquest palpable.

One of the lessons of CD is that many of the same preparations can be useful to prepare for both attack and natural hazards. Evacuation planning, stockpiling food and water to shelter in place, and hardening electric grids can be useful for many kinds of threats. Schools can use storm shelters (or CD bunkers, for those that still have them) to provide protection from active shooters.[79] A locality can adapt national programs for its own uses, depending on the threats and risks in that jurisdiction.[80] EMI can provide emergency managers the tools to prepare for multiple kinds of threats and hazards in an uncertain future. The history of EM shows that the threats and hazard environment change over time, even if there are long-term repeatable risks (e.g., flooding in low-lying areas).

Homeland defense and EM are distinct fields, but they share the goal of building national resilience. The homeland security and defense education and training ecosystem only partially overlaps EM. Most local emergency managers do not deal with nation-state threats or terrorist networks directly, but those threats command attention in homeland defense circles. However, both EM and homeland defense aim at building resilience within the borders of the United States. The March 2021 North American Aerospace Defense Command and U.S. Northern Command strategy makes building national resilience a core strategic goal to defend the United States against nation-state and other threats.[81] For their part, emergency managers help build national resilience by developing the core leadership and technical skills of their profession and enhancing resilience at the community level.

One major difference between the current institutional logic and the CD past is that CD and the EM planning that grew out of it were premised on the idea of warning. Many of the CDSC materials and early EM materials focused on digesting and communicating warning information and providing communities warning so that they could evacuate—whether they were fleeing hurricanes or a missile strike.[82] However, many of today's threats do not offer the luxury of warning; cyberattacks can close power grids instantaneously, infectious diseases circulate before they are identified, and hypersonic missiles travel at five times the speed of sound.[83] Climate change is associated with increasingly rapid onsets of storms and shortened evacuation timelines. Enhancing resilience and community lifelines and the ability to bounce back from a disaster might be the best preparation in an era in which warning time cannot be assured.

---

[77] Alan G. Stolberg, *How Nation-States Craft National Security Strategy Documents*, Strategic Studies Institute, U.S. Army War College, October 2012.

[78] EOP, *National Security Strategy of the United States of America*, White House, December 2017.

[79] James Tennent, "To Keep Students Safe, Oklahoma Is Using Bulletproof Storm Shelters at Elementary and Middle Schools," *Newsweek*, February 28, 2018.

[80] Roberts, 2014.

[81] James Redick and Glenn Jones, *The Need for an Integrated Strategy: Denial, Deterrence, and Relentless Resilience*, North American Aerospace Defense Command, undated; North American Aerospace Defense Command and U.S. Northern Command, "NORAD and USNORTHCOM Strategy: Executive Summary," March 15, 2021, p. 9.

[82] Daniel Byman, "Strategic Surprise and the September 11 Attacks," *Annual Review of Political Science*, Vol. 8, 2005, p. 145; Jack Davis, "Strategic Warning: Intelligence Support in a World of Uncertainty and Surprise," in Loch K. Johnson, ed., *Handbook of Intelligence Studies*, Routledge, 2007.

[83] Janet Loehrke and George Petras, "Visual Explainer: How China's Hypersonic Missile Compares to Conventional Ballistic Weapons," *USA Today*, November 4, 2021.

APPENDIX

Methods and Data Limitations

Review of Documents

This report's analysis drew on scholarly literature, as well as government and research organization reports and documents. Relevant scholarly literature was identified through keyword searches using Google Scholar and EBSCO Academic Search Complete. Keywords included the following words and their roots (to account for variations, such as plural forms): *civil defense*; *emergency management*; *Civil Defense Staff College*; *Emergency Management Institute*; and *Emmitsburg, MD*. These searches returned more than 1,000 documents, which were narrowed to a group of approximately 400 that were deemed relevant to the research questions and were reviewed more closely. After reviewing these documents, the research team reviewed additional documents deemed relevant that were cited in the footnotes of the core group of 400.

In addition, I used my knowledge of CD and EM history to consult major histories of events and organizations during the period studied. RAND readers of the report suggested additional literature to review and incorporate into the report.

Finally, I reviewed numerous government documents available through the EMI, FEMA, and DHS websites. In addition, the research assistants and I searched for mentions of CDSC and EMI in GAO reports, congressional hearings, the online catalog of the Civil Defense Museum, and the online catalog of the Carter, Reagan, George H. W. Bush, George W. Bush, and Clinton libraries. Finally, the team reviewed FCDA annual reports, EMI annual reports, and budget and personnel data found in these reports or provided by EMI.

Interviews and Discussions

I relied primarily on documentary evidence, supplemented by discussions and interviews. I had multiple discussions with the project sponsor team, which consisted of seven current officials from EMI. Although this is a documentary history, not an oral one, I sought out individuals beyond the sponsor team who could provide context for the documents, in the manner of an informant in anthropological research.[1] I identified ten people for interviews, and five of those responded and agreed to interviews. All of these were influential actors in EMI's history who were known to still be active in professional circles (even if some were formally retired). These include senior leaders who served in both CDSC and EMI, as well as former EMI superintendents. Those who did not respond did not explicitly refuse, but they were not available after multiple attempts to contact them.

The interviews were conducted via Microsoft Teams or phone and lasted approximately an hour to an hour and a half. Interview teams consisted of one to two interviewers and a notetaker. Interviewees were promised nonattribution, and anyone quoted by name in this report is quoted from public documents.

[1] Bernard et al., 1984.

The interview questions addressed the background of the respondent, the mission of EMI, the EMI student population, interactions with other organizations outside of EMI, the EM profession, and challenges faced by EMI during the interviewees' period of involvement. Although the number of interviews is limited, these interviews provided valuable context for evidence found in documents.

Data Sources for Emergency Management Institute Budgets and Courses

Data sources used for EMI budgets, enrollments, and courses in Chapter 1 have some limitations. For any year for which no data were available, figures show a grayed-out year with no bar chart. For 1951 through 1974, budget data include programs in the parent organization education and training budget that were not strictly part of CDSC. These include the Civil Defense Adult Education Program and the Civil Defense University Extension Program. These programs worked hand in hand with CDSC, and it was not possible to disaggregate their budgets from that of CDSC given available data. Beginning in 1969, budget limitations led to reductions in these programs, which affect the overall budget totals.[2]

No budget data are available for 1974 through 1995. It is possible that EMI's budget was assembled from multiple sources during that period and there was not a practice of issuing an annual report. In addition, only limited course and enrollment data were available for 1974 through 1981, which was a period of churn for EMI.

Resident course offering and enrollment data do not tell the full story, either. Throughout its history, EMI offered courses at locations other than its main campus and through mail and, later, video and online. The number of nonresident courses is far greater than the number of courses offered on campus. Some nonresident courses are instructor-led, and some are self-study and self-paced. Therefore, the number of resident courses does not tell the full story of EMI's reach and impact. For resident courses, EMI shared housing facilities with NFA beginning in 1981. Space for EMI students sometimes depended on NFA needs.

The data are shaded according to the era or institutional logic of the period, which is explained in further detail in the report. The CD era had larger budgets than other eras, and the budget includes many nonresidential programs that declined after 1969 and were not included in budget totals after 1979 even if similar functions were performed elsewhere in FEMA. The EM and homeland security eras in orange and blue show a steady increase in courses and graduates.

Data Sources for Emergency Management Institute Higher Education Programs Count

The number of FEMA higher education programs described in Chapter 5 relied on multiple data sources. The original list was created and kept by Blanchard, but a full list required gathering data from multiple sources, including the following:

- Bennett, 2017
- Bennett, 2018
- Bennett, 2020
- Blanchard, 2003

[2] OCD, 1969, p. 114.

- Blanchard, 2022
- Cwiak, 2008
- Cwiak, 2009
- Cwiak, 2012
- Cwiak, 2014
- Cwiak, 2015
- Cwiak, 2016
- EMI, 2021
- FEMA, undated.

Abbreviations

CD	civil defense
CDP	Center for Domestic Preparedness
CDSC	Civil Defense Staff College
CEM	comprehensive emergency management
CERT	Community Emergency Response Team
CHDS	Center for Homeland Defense and Security
COVID-19	coronavirus disease 2019
CSTI	California Specialized Training Institute
DCPA	Defense Civil Preparedness Agency
DHS	U.S. Department of Homeland Security
DoD	U.S. Department of Defense
EM	emergency management
EMI	Emergency Management Institute
EO	executive order
EOP	Executive Office of the President
FCDA	Federal Civil Defense Administration
FEMA	Federal Emergency Management Agency
FY	fiscal year
GAO	U.S. Government Accountability Office
IAEM	International Association of Emergency Managers
ICS	incident command system
IEMC	integrated emergency management course
NEMA	National Emergency Management Association
NETC	National Emergency Training Center
NFA	National Fire Academy
NIC	National Integration Center
NIMS	National Incident Management System
OCD	Office of Civil Defense
OCDM	Office of Civil and Defense Mobilization
OEP	Office of Emergency Planning
PD	presidential directive
QHSR	Quadrennial Homeland Security Review
SEPC	Senior Executive Policy Center
SLTT	state, local, tribal, and territorial
USFA	U.S. Fire Administration
USSR	Union of Soviet Socialist Republics
WMD	weapon of mass destruction

Bibliography

"A House Panel Has Recommended That the Justice Department . . .," United Press International, July 26, 1985.

Amdam, Rolv Petter, "Executive Education and the Managerial Revolution: The Birth of Executive Education at Harvard Business School," *Business History Review*, Vol. 90, No. 4, 2017.

Analyst in American national government, *Presidential Reorganization Authority: History, Recent Initiatives, and Options for Congress*, Congressional Research Service, R42852, December 11, 2012.

Analyst in emergency management policy, *The National Response Framework: Overview and Possible Issues for Congress*, Congressional Research Service, RL34758, January 21, 2011.

Andrews, Rhys, and Tom Entwistle, "Does Cross-Sectoral Partnership Deliver? An Empirical Exploration of Public Service Effectiveness, Efficiency, and Equity," *Journal of Public Administration Research and Theory*, Vol. 20, No. 3, July 2010.

Aspin, Les, "The 'Mineshaft Gap Revisited: Soviet Civil Defense and U.S. Deterrence," unpublished manuscript, December 1977.

Barnes, Michael D., Carl L. Hanson, Len M. B. Novilla, Aaron T. Meacham, Emily McIntyre, and Brittany C. Erickson, "Analysis of Media Agenda Setting During and After Hurricane Katrina: Implications for Emergency Preparedness, Disaster Response, and Disaster Policy," *American Journal of Public Health*, Vol. 98, No. 4, April 2008.

Becker, Elizabeth, "Washington Talk: Prickly Roots of Homeland Security," *New York Times*, August 31, 2002.

Bellavita, Christopher, "Changing Homeland Security: What Is Homeland Security?" *Homeland Security Affairs*, Vol. 4, June 2008.

Bennett, DeeDee, *Emergency Management Programs in Higher Education: Status*, Federal Emergency Management Agency, U.S. Department of Homeland Security, 2017.

Bennett, DeeDee, *Emergency Management Programs in Higher Education: Status Update—2018 FEMA Higher Education Program Report*, Federal Emergency Management Agency, U.S. Department of Homeland Security, June 2018.

Bennett, DeeDee, *2020 FEMA Higher Education State of the Community: Annual Survey and Report*, Federal Emergency Management Agency, U.S. Department of Homeland Security, circa 2020.

Berggren, Caroline, and Nathanael Lauster, "The Motherhood Penalty and the Professional Credential: Inequality in Career Development for Those with Professional Degrees," *International Studies in Sociology of Education*, Vol. 24, No. 1, 2014.

Bernard, H. Russell, Peter Killworth, David Kronenfeld, and Lee Sailer, "The Problem of Informant Accuracy: The Validity of Retrospective Data," *Annual Review of Anthropology*, Vol. 13, October 1984.

Birkland, Thomas A., "Focusing Events, Mobilization, and Agenda Setting," *Journal of Public Policy*, Vol. 18, No. 1, January–April 1998.

Blanchard, Wayne, "Compilation of Outlines and Syllabi of Emergency Management–Related College Courses," Emergency Management Institute, May 25, 1995.

Blanchard, B. Wayne, "The New Role of Higher Education in Emergency Management," *Journal of Emergency Management*, Vol. 1, No. 2, 2003.

Blanchard, B. Wayne, "Top Ten Competencies for Professional Emergency Management," October 7, 2005.

Blanchard, Wayne, "FEMA Emergency Management Higher Education Project Update," remarks made at the Emergency Management and Homeland Security/Defense Higher Education Conference, June 2006.

Blanchard, B. Wayne, "Higher Education Program Overview: Framing the Future," briefing slides, presented at 11th annual Federal Emergency Management Agency Emergency Management Higher Education Conference, June 2–8, 2008.

Blanchard, B. Wayne, "Changes in Collegiate Emergency Management and H.S. Programs During 2003," from the Federal Emergency Management Agency Emergency Management Institute Higher Education Program archive via email from Barbara Jones, July 12, 2022.

Blazich, Frank A., Jr., "Accelerated Action: The North Carolina Civil Defense Agency and the Cuban Missile Crisis, October–December 1962," *North Carolina Historical Review*, Vol. 86, No. 1, January 2009.

Bosher, Lee, Ksenia Chmutina, and Dewald van Niekerk, "Stop Going Around in Circles: Towards a Reconceptualisation of Disaster Risk Management Phases," *Disaster Prevention and Management*, Vol. 30, No. 4–5, 2021.

Brown, George E., Jr., "Mayor Tom Bradley Attends the Federal Emergency Management Agency's Integrated Emergency Management Course," *Congressional Record*, Vol. 130, Part 7, April 25, 1984. As of October 28, 2022: https://www.congress.gov/bound-congressional-record/1984/04/25/extensions-of-remarks-section

Bush, George W., "Management of Domestic Incidents," Homeland Security Presidential Directive 5, February 28, 2003.

Byman, Daniel, "Strategic Surprise and the September 11 Attacks," *Annual Review of Political Science*, Vol. 8, 2005.

Carter, Jimmy, "Federal Emergency Management Agency Remarks Announcing Reorganization Plan No. 3 of 1978," June 19, 1978a.

Carter, Jimmy, "U.S. Civil Defense Policy (U)," White House, Presidential Directive 41, September 29, 1978b.

Carter, Jimmy, "Federal Emergency Management Agency," White House, Executive Order 12127, March 31, 1979a.

Carter, Jimmy, "Emergency Management Agency," White House, Executive Order 12148, July 20, 1979b.

Carter, Jimmy, "President's Commission on the Accident at Three Mile Island Remarks Announcing Actions in Response to the Commission's Report," December 7, 1979c.

Center for Homeland Defense and Security, Naval Postgraduate School, "About CHDS," webpage, undated. As of July 7, 2022:
https://www.chds.us/c/about-chds/

Center for Homeland Defense and Security, "University and Agency Partnership Initiative," brochure, 2016.

Cha, Victor, and Katrin Fraser Katz, "The Burgeoning North Korea Missile Threat," Center for Strategic and International Studies, April 29, 2022.

CHDS—*See* Center for Homeland Defense and Security.

Chemical Stockpile Emergency Preparedness Program, homepage, undated. As of July 7, 2022: https://www.cseppportal.net

Chipman, William, *Civil Defense for the 1980's: Current Issues*, Defense Civil Preparedness Agency, white paper, July 13, 1979.

Chipman, William K., "Putting the 'DUAL' Back into Dual-Use Civil Defense," *Journal of Civil Defense*, June 1989.

Civil Defense Museum, "Civil Defense Art Gallery," webpage, undated-a. As of November 10, 2022: http://www.civildefensemuseum.com/artgal/artgallery.html

Civil Defense Museum, history webpage, undated-b. As of July 12, 2022: http://www.civildefensemuseum.com/history.html

Clinton, William J., "Report on Government Capabilities to Respond to Terrorist Incidents Involving Weapons of Mass Destruction: Message from the President of the United States," *Congressional Record*, Vol. 143, No. 22, February 26, 1997.

Code of Federal Regulations, Title 44, Emergency Management and Assistance; Chapter I, Federal Emergency Management Agency, Department of Homeland Security; Subchapter F, Preparedness; Part 350, Review and Approval of State and Local Radiological Emergency Plans and Preparedness.

Code of Federal Regulations, Title 44, Emergency Management and Assistance; Chapter I, Federal Emergency Management Agency, Department of Homeland Security; Subchapter F, Preparedness; Part 351, Radiological Emergency Planning and Preparedness.

Code of Federal Regulations, Title 44, Emergency Management and Assistance; Chapter I, Federal Emergency Management Agency, Department of Homeland Security; Subchapter F, Preparedness; Part 352, Commercial Nuclear Power Plants: Emergency Preparedness Planning.

Collier, Stephen J., and Andrew Lakoff, *The Government of Emergency: Vital Systems, Expertise, and the Politics of Security*, Princeton University Press, 2021.

Comfort, Louise K., William L. Waugh, and Beverly A. Cigler, "Emergency Management Research and Practice in Public Administration: Emergence, Expansion, and Future Directions," *Public Administration Review*, Vol. 72, No. 4, July–August 2012.

Committee on Banking, Housing, and Urban Affairs, U.S. Senate, *Civil Defense*, hearing on oversight on the role of civil defense in the United States–Soviet strategic balance, the effectiveness of existing Soviet and U.S. programs, and the feasibility of passive defenses for the survival of the population and the economy, 95th Cong., 2nd Sess., January 8, 1979.

Committee on Homeland Security, U.S. House of Representatives, *The Challenge of Protecting Mass Gatherings in a Post-9/11 World*, hearing, 110th Con., 2nd Sess., July 9, 2008.

Committee on Homeland Security and Governmental Affairs, U.S. Senate, *Hurricane Katrina: The Roles of U.S. Department of Homeland Security and Federal Emergency Management Agency Leadership*, hearing, 109th Cong., 2nd Sess., February 10, 2006.

Committee on Indian Affairs, U.S. Senate, *Emergency Management in Indian Country: Improving FEMA's Federal–Tribal Relationship with Indian Tribes*, hearing, 115th Cong., 1st Sess., February 8, 2017.

Committee on Oversight and Government Reform, U.S. House of Representatives, *FEMA Preparedness in 2007 and Beyond*, hearing, 110th Cong., 1st Sess., July 31, 2007.

Connecticut State Commission on Fire Prevention and Control, "2003 Harvard Fire Executive Fellowship Program," webpage, undated. As of October 28, 2022:
https://portal.ct.gov/CFPC/_old/News/Announcements/2003-Harvard-Fire-Executive-Fellowship-Program

Cooper, Christopher, and Robert Block, *Disaster: Hurricane Katrina and the Failure of Homeland Security*, Times Books, 2007.

Crompton, Rosemary, and Kay Sanderson, "Credentials and Careers: Some Implications of the Increase in Professional Qualifications Amongst Women," *Sociology*, Vol. 20, No. 1, February 1986.

Cutter, Susan L., Christopher T. Emrich, Jerry T. Mitchell, Bryan J. Boruff, Melanie Gall, Mathew C. Schmidtlein, Christopher G. Burton, and Ginni Melton, "The Long Road Home: Race, Class, and Recovery from Hurricane Katrina," *Environment: Science and Policy for Sustainable Development*, Vol. 48, No. 2, 2006.

Cwiak, Carol, *Emergency Management Education: A Status Report—2008 FEMA Emergency Management Higher Education Program Report*, Federal Emergency Management Agency, U.S. Department of Homeland Security, 2008.

Cwiak, Carol, North Dakota State University, *Emergency Management Education: A Snapshot of the Community—2009 FEMA Emergency Management Higher Education Program Report*, briefing slides, circa 2009.

Cwiak, Carol, "Framing the Future: What Should Emergency Management Graduates Know?" *Journal of Homeland Security and Emergency Management*, Vol. 8, No. 2, 2011.

Cwiak, Carol, *Shaping the Future: A Status Report on Emergency Management Higher Education*, Federal Emergency Management Agency Higher Education Program report, 2012.

Cwiak, Carol L., "Emergency Management Higher Education Today: The 2014 FEMA Higher Education Program Survey," Federal Emergency Management Agency, U.S. Department of Homeland Security, 2014.

Cwiak, Carol L., *Advancing Higher Education Efforts: 2015 FEMA Higher Education Program Report*, Federal Emergency Management Agency, U.S. Department of Homeland Security, circa 2015.

Cwiak, Carol, "Emergency Management Higher Education: Where Do We Stand? 2016 FEMA Higher Education Program Survey," briefing slides, Federal Emergency Management Agency, U.S. Department of Homeland Security, circa 2016.

Daniels, R. Steven, and Carolyn L. Clark-Daniels, *Transforming Government: The Renewal and Revitalization of the Federal Emergency Management Agency*, PricewaterhouseCoopers Endowment for the Business of Government, April 2000.

Daniels, R. Steven, and Carolyn L. Clark-Daniels, "Transforming the Federal Emergency Management Agency: The Renewal and Revitalization of FEMA," in Mark A. Abramson and Paul R. Lawrence, eds., *Transforming Organizations*, Rowman and Littlefield Publishers, 2001.

Data USA, "Emergency Management Directors," webpage, undated. As of July 7, 2022:
https://datausa.io/profile/soc/emergency-management-directors

Davis, Jack, "Strategic Warning: Intelligence Support in a World of Uncertainty and Surprise," in Loch K. Johnson, ed., *Handbook of Intelligence Studies*, Routledge, 2007.

DCPA—*See* Defense Civil Preparedness Agency.

Defense Civil Preparedness Agency, U.S. Department of Defense, *Civil Preparedness: A New Dual Mission—Annual Report Fiscal Year 1972*, December 15, 1972.

Defense Civil Preparedness Agency, U.S. Department of Defense, *Foresight: Annual Report FY 1973*, February 8, 1974.

Defense Civil Preparedness Agency, U.S. Department of Defense, *Taking Measure: Annual Report 1975*, June 30, 1975.

Defense Production Act—*See* Public Law 81-774.

Dempsey, John R., "Carter Reorganization: A Midterm Appraisal," *Public Administration Review*, Vol. 39, No. 1, January–February 1979.

Department of Political Science, College of Liberal Arts, Auburn University, "ePortfolio," webpage, undated. As of October 28, 2022:
https://cla.auburn.edu/polisci/master-of-public-administration/curriculum/eportfolio/

De Witte, Melissa, "How Stanford Scholars Are Teaching the Next Generation About 9/11," *Stanford News*, September 8, 2021.

DHS—*See* U.S. Department of Homeland Security.

Disaster Relief Act of 1950—*See* Public Law 81-875.

Disaster Relief Act of 1974—*See* Public Law 93-288.

Doughty, Robert A., *The Command and General Staff College in Transition, 1946–1976*, U.S. Army Command and General Staff College, June 11, 1976.

Drabek, Thomas E., "The Professional Emergency Manager: Structures and Strategies for Success," in *The Professional Emergency Manager: Structures and Strategies for Success*, Institute of Behavioral Science, University of Colorado, 1987.

Drabek, Thomas E., "Emergency Management and Homeland Security Curricula: Contexts, Cultures, and Constraints," *Journal of Emergency Management*, Vol. 5, No. 5, 2007a.

Drabek, Thomas E., *Social Problems Perspectives, Disaster Research and Emergency Management: Intellectual Contexts, Theoretical Extensions, and Policy Implications*, revision and expansion of the E. L. Quarantelli Award Lecture, Emergency Management Institute, Federal Emergency Management Agency, August 2007b.

DRI International, "Certified Business Continuity Professional (CBCP)," webpage, undated. As of October 29, 2022:
https://drii.org/certification/cbcp

Dynes, Russell R., "Problems in Emergency Planning," *Energy*, Vol. 8, No. 8–9, August–September 1983.

Eiben, Carole, and Bruce Marshall, "EENET: Emergency Education NETwork," edited version of July 8, 1998, online presentation for Emergency Information Infrastructure Partnership, circa 1998.

Ellis, Ryan, *Letters, Power Lines, and Other Dangerous Things: The Politics of Infrastructure Security*, Massachusetts Institute of Technology Press, 2020.

Emergency Management Institute, Federal Emergency Management Agency, *Course Catalog, 1983–1984*, National Emergency Training Center, c. 1983.

Emergency Management Institute, Federal Emergency Management Agency, *Course Catalog 1984–1985*, c. 1984.

Emergency Management Institute, Federal Emergency Management Agency, *Course Catalog 1986–1987*, c. 1986.

Emergency Management Institute, Federal Emergency Management Agency, "1987–88 Schedule of Courses," National Emergency Training Center, c. 1987.

Emergency Management Institute, Federal Emergency Management Agency, *1988/89 Catalog of Activities*, c. 1988.

Emergency Management Institute, Federal Emergency Management Agency, *1989/90 Catalog of Activities*, c. 1989.

Emergency Management Institute, Federal Emergency Management Agency, *Catalog of Activities/1991–1992*, c. 1991.

Emergency Management Institute, Federal Emergency Management Agency, *Catalog of Activities 1992–1993*, c. 1992.

Emergency Management Institute, Federal Emergency Management Agency, *Catalog of Activities 1993–1994*, c. 1993.

Emergency Management Institute, Federal Emergency Management Agency, *Catalog of Activities 1994–1995*, c. 1994.

Emergency Management Institute, Federal Emergency Management Agency, *Catalog of Activities 1995–1996*, c. 1995.

Emergency Management Institute, Federal Emergency Management Agency, *Catalog of Activities 1996–1997*, c. 1996.

Emergency Management Institute, Federal Emergency Management Agency, *Catalog of Activities 1997–1998*, c. 1997.

Emergency Management Institute, Federal Emergency Management Agency, *Catalog of Activities 1998–1999*, c. 1998.

Emergency Management Institute, Federal Emergency Management Agency, *Catalog of Activities 1999–2000*, c. 1999.

Emergency Management Institute, Federal Emergency Management Agency, *Catalog of Activities 2000–2001*, c. 2000.

Emergency Management Institute, Federal Emergency Management Agency, *Catalog of Activities 2001–2002*, c. 2001.

Emergency Management Institute, Federal Emergency Management Agency, *Catalog of Activities 2002–2003*, c. 2002.

Emergency Management Institute, Federal Emergency Management Agency, U.S. Department of Homeland Security, *FY 2008 Annual Report*, 2008.

Emergency Management Institute, Federal Emergency Management Agency, U.S. Department of Homeland Security, *FY 2009 EMI Annual Report*, 2009.

Emergency Management Institute, Federal Emergency Management Agency, U.S. Department of Homeland Security, *Fiscal Year 2010 Annual Report*, December 28, 2011.

Emergency Management Institute, Federal Emergency Management Agency, U.S. Department of Homeland Security, *Fiscal Year 2012 Training Catalog*, 2012a.

Emergency Management Institute, Federal Emergency Management Agency, U.S. Department of Homeland Security, *Fiscal Year 2011 Annual Report*, May 29, 2012b.

Emergency Management Institute, Federal Emergency Management Agency, U.S. Department of Homeland Security, *Fiscal Year 2012 Annual Report*, May 1, 2013.

Emergency Management Institute, Federal Emergency Management Agency, U.S. Department of Homeland Security, "Emergency Management Institute Mission," webpage, last modified December 1, 2014. As of October 29, 2022:
https://training.fema.gov/mission.aspx

Emergency Management Institute, Federal Emergency Management Agency, U.S. Department of Homeland Security, *FY 2015 Annual Report*, 2015.

Emergency Management Institute, Federal Emergency Management Agency, U.S. Department of Homeland Security, *Annual Report Fiscal Year 2017*, 2017.

Emergency Management Institute, Federal Emergency Management Agency, U.S. Department of Homeland Security, *Fiscal Year 2018 Annual Report*, 2018.

Emergency Management Institute, Federal Emergency Management Agency, U.S. Department of Homeland Security, *Annual Report Draft*, 2019a.

Emergency Management Institute, Federal Emergency Management Agency, U.S. Department of Homeland Security, *Fiscal Year 2019 Annual Report*, 2019b.

Emergency Management Institute, Federal Emergency Management Agency, U.S. Department of Homeland Security, "Emergency Management Institute (EMI) Overview," webpage, last modified October 16, 2019c. As of October 29, 2022:
https://training.fema.gov/history.aspx

Emergency Management Institute, Federal Emergency Management Agency, U.S. Department of Homeland Security, *Emergency Management Institute FY 2019 Annual Report*, draft, 2020.

Emergency Management Institute, Federal Emergency Management Agency, U.S. Department of Homeland Security, *Monthly Newsletter*, Vol. 1, No. 6, June 8, 2021.

Emergency Management Institute, Federal Emergency Management Agency, U.S. Department of Homeland Security, "List of Superintendents," 2022.

EMI—*See* Emergency Management Institute.

Enarson, Elaine, and Betty Hearn Morrow, *The Gendered Terrain of Disaster: Through Women's Eyes*, Praeger, 1998.

EO 12127—*See* Carter, 1979a.

EO 12148—*See* Carter, 1979b.

EOP—*See* Executive Office of the President.

Erikson, Kai T., *Everything in Its Path: Destruction of Community in the Buffalo Creek Flood*, Simon and Schuster, 1976.

Executive Office of the President, *National Security Strategy of the United States of America*, White House, December 2017.

Farris, David, and Robert McCreight, "The Professionalization of Emergency Management in Institutions of Higher Education," *Journal of Homeland Security and Emergency Management*, Vol. 11, No. 1, 2014.

FCDA—*See* Federal Civil Defense Administration.

Federal Civil Defense Act of 1950—*See* Public Law 81-920.

Federal Civil Defense Administration, *Annual Report for 1951 of the Federal Civil Defense Administration to the President and the Congress of the United States of America*, April 18, 1952.

Federal Civil Defense Administration, *Annual Report for 1952*, 1953.

Federal Civil Defense Administration, *Annual Report for 1953*, 1954.

Federal Civil Defense Administration, *Annual Report for 1954*, 1955.

Federal Civil Defense Administration, *Annual Report for 1955*, 1956.

Federal Civil Defense Administration, *Annual Report for Fiscal Year 1956*, 1957.

Federal Civil Defense Administration, *Annual Report for Fiscal Year 1957*, 1958.

Federal Emergency Management Agency, U.S. Department of Homeland Security, "The FEMA Higher Education College List," webpage, undated. As of November 12, 2022: https://training.fema.gov/hiedu/collegelist/

Federal Emergency Management Agency, "Welcome to the National Emergency Training Center," FEMA-12, October 1981.

Federal Emergency Management Agency, *Report from the Training and Fire Programs Directorate*, 1983.

Federal Emergency Management Agency, U.S. Department of Homeland Security, *Three Mile Island Generating Station Exercise: April 14, 2009*, June 19, 2009.

Federal Emergency Management Agency, U.S. Department of Homeland Security, *A Whole Community Approach to Emergency Management: Principles, Themes, and Pathways for Action*, FDOC 104-008-1, December 2011.

Federal Emergency Management Agency, U.S. Department of Homeland Security, *Budget Overview: Fiscal Year 2018 Congressional Justification*, c. 2017.

Federal Emergency Management Agency, U.S. Department of Homeland Security, *Budget Overview: Fiscal Year 2019 Congressional Justification*, c. 2018a.

Federal Emergency Management Agency, U.S. Department of Homeland Security, "NIMS Implementation Objectives for Local, State, Tribal, and Territorial Jurisdictions: 2018 Update," c. 2018b.

Federal Emergency Management Agency, U.S. Department of Homeland Security, *Budget Overview: Fiscal Year 2020 Congressional Justification*, c. 2019a.

Federal Emergency Management Agency, U.S. Department of Homeland Security, *National Response Framework*, 4th ed., October 28, 2019b.

Federal Emergency Management Agency, U.S. Department of Homeland Security, *Budget Overview: Fiscal Year 2021 Congressional Justification*, c. 2020a.

Federal Emergency Management Agency, U.S. Department of Homeland Security, "Community Lifelines," webpage, last updated July 27, 2020b. As of July 7, 2022: https://www.fema.gov/emergency-managers/practitioners/lifelines

Federal Emergency Management Agency, U.S. Department of Homeland Security, "IEMC: Community-Specific," webpage, last updated November 3, 2020c. As of July 7, 2022: https://training.fema.gov/iemc/communityspec.aspx

Federal Emergency Management Agency, U.S. Department of Homeland Security, *Budget Overview: Fiscal Year 2022 Congressional Justification*, c. 2021a.

Federal Emergency Management Agency, U.S. Department of Homeland Security, "Disaster Authorities," webpage, last updated July 6, 2021b. As of July 7, 2022: https://www.fema.gov/disaster/authorities

Federal Emergency Management Agency, U.S. Department of Homeland Security, "FEMA's Higher Education Articles and Papers," webpage, October 25, 2021c. As of July 7, 2022: http://training.fema.gov/EMIWeb/edu/highpapers.asp

Federal Emergency Management Agency, U.S. Department of Homeland Security, *2022–2026 FEMA Strategic Plan: Building the FEMA Our Nation Needs and Deserves*, circa December 16, 2021d.

Federal Emergency Management Agency, U.S. Department of Homeland Security, *Budget Overview: Fiscal Year 2023 Congressional Justification*, c. March 2022a.

Federal Emergency Management Agency, U.S. Department of Homeland Security, "Emergency Management Professional Program (EMPP)," webpage, last modified May 23, 2022b. As of November 12, 2022: https://training.fema.gov/empp/

Federal Emergency Management Agency, U.S. Department of Homeland Security, "The National Emergency Management Executive Academy," webpage, last modified May 23, 2022c. As of July 7, 2022: https://training.fema.gov/empp/executive.aspx

Federal Emergency Management Agency, U.S. Department of Homeland Security, "About FEMA," webpage, last updated June 7, 2022d. As of October 29, 2022: https://www.fema.gov/about

Federal Emergency Management Agency, U.S. Department of Homeland Security, "Higher Education Program," webpage, last updated June 14, 2022e. As of July 7, 2022: https://training.fema.gov/hiedu

Federal Emergency Management Agency, U.S. Department of Homeland Security, "Training and Education," website, last updated July 14, 2022f. As of October 29, 2022: https://www.fema.gov/emergency-managers/national-preparedness/training

Federal Emergency Management Agency, U.S. Department of Homeland Security, "Tribal Affairs," webpage, last updated September 8, 2022g. As of July 7, 2022: https://www.fema.gov/about/organization/tribes

Federal Emergency Management Agency and U.S. Nuclear Regulatory Commission, "Memoranda of Understanding Between Federal Emergency Management Agency and Nuclear Regulatory Commission," *Federal Register*, Vol. 45, No. 243, December 16, 1980.

Fekete, Alexander, Gabriele Hufschmidt, and Sylvia Kruse, "Benefits and Challenges of Resilience and Vulnerability for Disaster Risk Management," *International Journal of Disaster Risk Science*, Vol. 5, No. 1, March 2014.

Feldmann-Jensen, Shirley, Steven J. Jensen, Sandy Maxwell Smith, and Gregory Vigneaux, "The Next Generation Core Competencies for Emergency Management," *Journal of Emergency Management* (Weston, Mass.), Vol. 17, No. 1, January–February 2019.

FEMA—*See* Federal Emergency Management Agency.

FEMA 2022–2026 strategic plan—*See* Federal Emergency Management Agency, 2021c.

"FEMA's Gaynor to Emergency Managers Requesting Action on Critical Steps," *Government Technology and Services Coalition Homeland Security Today*, March 28, 2020. As of November 4, 2022: https://www.hstoday.us/subject-matter-areas/coronavirus/femas-gaynor-to-emergency-managers-requesting-action-on-critical-steps/

Finucane, Melissa L., Linnea Warren May, and Joan Chang, *A Scoping Literature Review on Indicators and Metrics for Assessing Racial Equity in Disaster Preparation, Response, and Recovery*, RAND Corporation, RR-A1083-1, 2021. As of October 29, 2022: https://www.rand.org/pubs/research_reports/RRA1083-1.html

Ford, John, Federal Emergency Management Agency, U.S. Department of Homeland Security, presentation at All-Hazards Incident Management Team Symposium, December 2018.

Frank, Thomas, "Disaster Management Is Too White, Official Tells Congress," *Scientific American E&E News*, July 29, 2020.

GAO—*See* U.S. Government Accountability Office.

Garrison, Dee, *Bracing for Armageddon: Why Civil Defense Never Worked*, Oxford University Press, 2006.

Gasco, Susan, "Three Things to Protect: Our Past, Present, and Future," National Emergency Management Advanced Academy paper, August 2019.

Geist, Edward, *Armageddon Insurance: Civil Defense in the United States and Soviet Union, 1945–1991*, University of North Carolina Press, 2019.

Goss, Kay C., visiting professor of political science, executive in residence, and interim director for international studies, University of Arkansas, biography, undated.

Gostin, Lawrence O., and Jennifer B. Nuzzo, "Twenty Years After the Anthrax Terrorist Attacks of 2001: Lessons Learned and Unlearned for the COVID-19 Response," *JAMA Network Open*, Vol. 326, No. 20, 2021.

Grossman, Andrew D., *Neither Dead nor Red: Civil Defense and American Political Development During the Early Cold War*, Routledge, 2002.

Hall, John, "Is Thought Leadership Everything It's Cracked Up to Be?" *Forbes*, November 3, 2019.

Hardy, Cynthia, "How Institutions Communicate; or How Does Communicating Institutionalize?" *Management Communication Quarterly*, Vol. 25, No. 1, 2011.

Haveman, Heather A., and Gillian Gualtieri, "Institutional Logics," *Oxford Research Encyclopedia of Business and Management*, Oxford University Press, January 19, 2017.

"Head of Disaster Relief Agency, Targeted in Inquiries, Resigns," *Los Angeles Times*, July 25, 1985.

Heyman, David, and James Jay Carafano, *Homeland Security 3.0: Building a National Enterprise to Keep America Safe, Free, and Prosperous*, Heritage Foundation Special Report, Center for Strategic and International Studies, SR-23, September 18, 2008.

Hickethier, Dennis, "The Virtual Campus for the National Emergency Training Center (NETC)," Emergency Information Infrastructure Partnership Virtual Forum presentation, April 2, 2003.

Hickethier, Dennis, Sue Mettlen, and Richard Muth, "Experiences with Distance Learning via the Internet," Emergency Information Infrastructure Partnership Virtual Library online presentation, January 14, 1998.

"High-Level Jousting over Civil Defense," *Washington Post*, June 19, 1978.

Hillman, Michael, "A Short History of St. Joseph College," Emmitsburg Area Historical Society, webpage, undated. As of September 29, 2022:
https://www.emmitsburg.net/archive_list/articles/places/schools/st_joes_college_2.htm

Homeland Security Act—*See* Public Law 107-296.

Homeland Security Digital Library, "Timeline: Federal Civil Defense Act of 1950," webpage, undated. As of July 5, 2022:
https://www.hsdl.org/c/tl/federal-civil-defense-act-1950/

Homeland Security Presidential Directive 5—*See* Bush, 2003.

Horowitz, Andy, *Katrina: A History, 1915–2015*, Harvard University Press, 2020.

IAEM—*See* International Association of Emergency Managers.

Information Services Office, Defense Civil Preparedness Agency, *Significant Events in United States Civil Defense History List Chronologically, 1916–1974*, compiled February 7, 1975. As of November 4, 2022:
https://irp.fas.org/agency/dhs/fema/cd-chron.pdf

Institute for Diversity and Inclusion in Emergency Management, "Our Goals," webpage, undated. As of November 4, 2022:
https://i-diem.org/our-goals/

International Association of Emergency Managers, "History of IAEM," webpage, undated-a. As of November 4, 2022:
https://www.iaem.org/History-of-IAEM

International Association of Emergency Managers, "History of the IAEM Certification Program," webpage, undated-b. As of November 4, 2022:
https://www.iaem.org/certification/history-of-cem

International Association of Emergency Managers, "IAEM Code of Ethics and Professional Conduct," webpage, undated-c.

International Association of Emergency Managers, "Principles of Emergency Management Supplement," September 11, 2007.

Iowa Civil Defense Division, U.S. Department of Defense, *Civil Defense: Training and Education Catalog*, 1974.

Ireland, Lee, *The NFA-EMI Story*, Booksurge, 2008.

Jenkins, Philip, *Images of Terror: What We Can and Can't Know About Terrorism*, Aldine de Gruyter, 2003.

Jenkins, William O., Jr., director, homeland security and justice issues, U.S. Government Accountability Office, *Actions Taken to Implement the Post-Katrina Emergency Management Reform Act of 2006*, report for congressional requesters, GAO-09-59R, November 21, 2008.

Johnson, Bridget, "'Unrelenting' Disasters Compel FEMA to Take 'Deep Dive' into Assessing Future Workforce, Criswell Says," *Government Technology and Services Coalition Homeland Security Today*, June 16, 2022.

Kaufman, Leslie, Mira Rojanasakul, Hayley Warren, Jason Kao, Brittany Harris, and Prashant Gopal, "Mapping America's Underwater Real Estate: What Happens to Home Prices If Flood Maps Start Measuring Climate Change? Millions of Americans Are About to Find Out," *Bloomberg*, June 29, 2020.

Kneeland, Timothy W., *Playing Politics with Natural Disaster: Hurricane Agnes, the 1972 Election, and the Origins of FEMA*, Cornell University Press, 2020.

Knowles, Scott Gabriel, "Defending Philadelphia: A Historical Case Study of Civil Defense in the Early Cold War," *Public Works Management and Policy*, Vol. 11, No. 3, January 2007.

Krepinevich, Andrew, and Barry Watts, *The Last Warrior: Andrew Marshall and the Shaping of Modern American Defense Strategy*, Basic Books, 2015.

Kreps, Gary A., "The Federal Emergency Management System in the United States: Past and Present," *International Journal of Mass Emergencies and Disasters*, Vol. 8, No. 3, November 1990.

Krugler, David F., *This Is Only a Test: How Washington, D.C. Prepared for Nuclear War*, Palgrave Macmillan, 2006.

Kurtz, Howard, "Retired Military Policemen Troop into Highly Paid Agency Jobs," *Washington Post*, February 3, 1985.

Lanouette, William, "The Best Civil Defense May Be the Best—or Worst—Offense," *National Journal*, September 9, 1978.

Larsen, Randall J., and Ruth A. David, "Homeland Defense: Assumptions First, Strategy Second," *Homeland Security*, October 2000.

Lehrer, Eli, "On Working from Home," *National Affairs*, Summer 2022.

Lewis, David E., *The Politics of Presidential Appointments: Political Control and Bureaucratic Performance*, Princeton University Press, 2010.

Liu, Ting-An-Xu, G. Breck Wightman, Euipyo Lee, and Jordan Hunter, "Revisiting 'Big Questions' of Public Administration After COVID-19: A Systematic Review," *Asia Pacific Journal of Public Administration*, Vol. 43, No. 3, 2021.

Local, State, Tribal, and Federal Preparedness Task Force, *Perspective on Preparedness: Taking Stock Since 9/11—Report to Congress of the Local, State, Tribal, and Federal Preparedness Task Force*, September 2010.

Loehrke, Janet, and George Petras, "Visual Explainer: How China's Hypersonic Missile Compares to Conventional Ballistic Weapons," *USA Today*, November 4, 2021.

Lustick, Ian S., "Fractured Fairy Tale: The War on Terror and the Emperor's New Clothes," *Homeland Security Affairs*, Vol. 3, No. 1, 2007.

Lorber, Judith, "The Social Construction of Gender," in Estelle Disch, ed., *Reconstructing Gender: A Multicultural Anthology*, McGraw-Hill Higher Education, 1994.

Management, Operations and Support Services Division, National Emergency Training Center, *2014 Annual Report*, January 7, 2015.

Marcus, Leonard J., Barry C. Dorn, and Joseph M. Henderson, "Meta-Leadership and National Emergency Preparedness: A Model to Build Government Connectivity," *Biosecurity and Bioterrorism: Biodefense Strategy, Practice, and Science*, Vol. 4, No. 2, 2006.

Maryland Department of Planning, Projections and Data Analysis, "2010 Census Profile of General Population and Housing Characteristics," undated.

"Maryland Site Gets Nod for Academy," *International Fire Chief*, Vol. 45, No. 3, March 1979.

Maxwell, Evan, and Bill Farr, "Disaster Strikes Los Angeles: This Is a Test," *Los Angeles Times*, March 9, 1984.

Mayorkas, Alejandro, Secretary of Homeland Security, U.S. Department of Homeland Security, "Secretary Mayorkas Delivers Remarks on Operation Allies Welcome," September 3, 2021.

McAllister, Bill, "FEMA Officials Admit Response to Hugo Was Slow," *Washington Post*, October 6, 1989.

McEnaney, Laura, *Civil Defense Begins at Home: Militarization Meets Everyday Life in the Fifties*, Princeton University Press, 2000.

McLoughlin, David, "A Framework for Integrated Emergency Management," *Public Administration Review*, Vol. 45, January 1985.

Menand, Louis, *The Marketplace of Ideas: Reform and Resistance in the American University*, W. W. Norton and Company, 2010.

Meyer, John W., and Brian Rowan, "Institutionalized Organizations: Formal Structure as Myth and Ceremony," *American Journal of Sociology*, Vol. 83, No. 2, September 1977.

Mitchell, Donald W., *Civil Defense: Planning for Survival and Recovery*, Industrial College of the Armed Forces, 1966.

National Centers for Environmental Information, National Oceanic and Atmospheric Administration, "Billion-Dollar Weather and Climate Disasters," webpage, undated. As of July 7, 2022:
https://www.ncei.noaa.gov/access/billions/events/US/1980-2006

National Civil Defense Staff College, *Training in Civil Defense*, Federal Civil Defense Administration, 1951.

National Commission on Fire Prevention and Control, *America Burning: The Report of the National Commission on Fire Prevention and Control*, 1973.

National Council of Architectural Registration Boards, "AXP Portfolio," webpage, undated. As of November 4, 2022:
https://www.ncarb.org/gain-axp-experience/start-axp/record-experience/axp-portfolio

National Training and Education Division, National Preparedness Directorate, Federal Emergency Management Agency, U.S. Department of Homeland Security, "National Preparedness Course Catalog," webpage, undated. As of January 29, 2023:
https://www.firstrespondertraining.gov/frts/npccatalog?catalog=EMI

National Governors' Association, *1979 Emergency Preparedness Project: Final Report*, 1979.

National Preparedness Goal—*See* U.S. Department of Homeland Security, 2015.

National Weather Service, "Hurricane Hugo—September 21–22, 1989," webpage, undated. As of July 7, 2022:
https://www.weather.gov/chs/HurricaneHugo-Sep1989

NCTA—The Internet and Television Association, "The Future Is 10G," webpage, undated. As of November 4, 2022:
https://www.ncta.com/positions/the-future-of-superfast-internet

Neal, David M., and Brenda Phillips, "Female-Dominated Local Social Movement Organizations in Disaster-Threat Situations," in Guida West and Rhoda Lois Blumberg, eds., *Women and Social Protest*, Oxford University Press, 1990.

Neary, Lynn, "FEMA Director Michael Brown Resigns," National Public Radio, September 12, 2005.

Network of Schools of Public Policy, Affairs, and Administration Admissions Professionals Meeting, American University, June 23, 2022.

New York City Emergency Management, "Nuclear Preparedness PSA," video, July 11, 2022.

Nohrstedt, Daniel, "Explaining Mobilization and Performance of Collaborations in Routine Emergency Management," *Administration and Society*, Vol. 48, No. 2, March 2016.

North American Aerospace Defense Command and U.S. Northern Command, "NORAD and USNORTHCOM Strategy: Executive Summary," March 15, 2021.

North Dakota State University, "Dr. B. Wayne Blanchard Award for Academic Excellence in Emergency Management Higher Education," webpage, last updated June 2, 2022. As of July 7, 2022:
https://www.ndsu.edu/emgt/blanchard_award/

OCD—*See* Office of Civil Defense.

OCDM—*See* Office of Civil and Defense Mobilization.

O'Donnell, James M., and James V. Zaccor, *Organizational Relocation Plan Development: Two Case Histories*, Industrial Emergency Council, April 1985.

Office of Civil and Defense Mobilization, Executive Office of the President, *Annual Report of the Office of Civil and Defense Mobilization for Fiscal Year 1958*, 1959.

Office of Civil and Defense Mobilization, Executive Office of the President, *Annual Report of the Office of Civil and Defense Mobilization for Fiscal Year 1959*, 1960.

Office of Civil Defense, U.S. Department of Defense, *Annual Report of the Office of Civil Defense for Fiscal Year 1962*, 1962.

Office of Civil Defense, U.S. Department of Defense, *Annual Report of the Office of Civil Defense for Fiscal Year 1963*, 1963.

Office of Civil Defense, Office of the Secretary of the Army, U.S. Department of Defense, *Annual Report of the Office of Civil Defense for Fiscal Year 1964*, December 28, 1964.

Office of Civil Defense, Office of the Secretary of the Army, U.S. Department of Defense, *Annual Report of the Office of Civil Defense for Fiscal Year 1966*, 1966.

Office of Civil Defense, Office of the Secretary of the Army, U.S. Department of Defense, *Annual Report of the Office of Civil Defense for Fiscal Year 1967*, 1967.

Office of Civil Defense, Office of the Secretary of the Army, U.S. Department of Defense, *Annual Report of the Office of Civil Defense for Fiscal Year 1968*, 1968.

Office of Civil Defense, Office of the Secretary of the Army, U.S. Department of Defense, *Annual Report of the Office of Civil Defense for Fiscal Year 1969*, December 20, 1969.

Office of Communications and Public Affairs, University of South Carolina, "Scholarship, Research, and the Legacy of 9/11," webpage, updated September 9, 2021. As of November 11, 2022: https://sc.edu/uofsc/posts/2021/09/september-11-faculty-respond.php

Office of Justice Programs, U.S. Department of Justice, "Nunn–Lugar–Domenici Domestic Preparedness Program: Program Overview," fact sheet, September 2001.

Office of Standards Development, Founding U.S. Nuclear Regulatory Commission, *Regulatory Guide*, Vol. 88, 1985.

O'Leary, Lizzie, "Can FEMA Survive Climate Change?" *Slate*, July 8, 2022.

PD-41—*See* Carter, 1978b.

Peabody, John N., Jr., president, American Federation of Government Employees Local 1983, prepared statement for U.S. Senate Hearing 105-427 on U.S. House of Representatives Bill 2158 and U.S. Senate Bill 1034 on appropriations for the U.S. Department of Veterans Affairs, the U.S. Department of Housing and Urban Development, and independent agencies for fiscal year 1998, February 25, 1997.

Perry, Ronald W., "What Is a Disaster?" in Havidan Rodriguez, Enrico L. Quarantelli, and Russell R. Dynes, eds., *Handbook of Disaster Research*, Springer, 2006.

Perry, Ronald W., and E. L. Quarantelli, eds., *What Is a Disaster? New Answers to Old Questions*, Xlibris, 2005.

Petak, William J., "Emergency Management: A Challenge for Public Administration," *Public Administration Review*, Vol. 45, January 1985.

Phillips, Brenda, "Gender as a Variable in Emergency Response," in Robert C. Bolin, ed., *The Loma Prieta Earthquake: Studies of Short-Term Impacts*, Institute of Behavioral Science, University of Colorado, 1990.

Phillips, Brenda D., David M. Neal, and Gary R. Webb, *Introduction to Emergency Management*, CRC Press, 2012.

Phillips, Brenda D., David M. Neal, and Gary R. Webb, "The Next Generation of Emergency Managers and Disaster Scientists," in Brenda D. Phillips, David M. Neal, and Gary R. Webb, eds., *Introduction to Emergency Management and Disaster Science*, Routledge, 2021.

Post-Katrina Emergency Management Reform Act—*See* Public Law 109-295.

Preparedness Training and Exercises Directorate, Federal Emergency Management Agency, "Accomplishment of the Past, Visions of the Future," June 1998.

President's Commission on the Accident at Three Mile Island, *Report of the President's Commission on the Accident at Three Mile Island—The Need for Change: The Legacy at TMI, October 1979, Washington, D.C.*, Pergamon, 1980.

Public Law 80-235, National Security Act of 1947, July 26, 1947.

Public Law 81-774, Defense Production Act, September 8, 1950.

Public Law 81-875, Disaster Relief Act for 1950, September 30, 1950.

Public Law 81-920, Federal Civil Defense Act of 1950, January 12, 1951.

Public Law 93-288, Disaster Relief Act of 1974, May 22, 1974.

Public Law 100-707, Robert T. Stafford Disaster Relief and Emergency Assistance Act, November 23, 1988.

Public Law 93-498, Federal Fire Prevention and Control Act of 1974, October 29, 1974.

Public Law 100-707, Robert T. Stafford Disaster Relief and Emergency Assistance Act, November 23, 1988.

Public Law 107-296, Homeland Security Act of 2002, November 25, 2002.

Public Law 109-295, Department of Homeland Security Appropriations Act, 2007, October 4, 2006.

Public Law 113-2, Disaster Relief Appropriations, January 29, 2013.

Quarantelli, Enrico L., "The Early History of the Disaster Research Center," undated.

Quarantelli, Enrico L., "The Origins and Impact of Disaster Research," in Margaret R. O'Leary, ed., *The First 72 Hours: A Community Approach to Disaster Preparedness*, iUniverse, 2004.

Reagan, Ronald, "Nomination of Louis O. Giuffrida to Be Director of the Federal Emergency Management Agency," February 24, 1981.

Reay, Trish, and Candace Jones, "Qualitatively Capturing Institutional Logics," *Strategic Organization*, Vol. 14, No. 4, November 2016.

Redick, James, and Glenn Jones, *The Need for an Integrated Strategy: Denial, Deterrence, and Relentless Resilience*, North American Aerospace Defense Command, undated.

Reese, Shawn, *Defining Homeland Security: Analysis and Congressional Considerations*, Congressional Research Service, RL42462, version 6, January 8, 2013.

Riecker, Timothy M., "The Hawaii Saga," *The Contrarian Emergency Manager*, blog post, January 31, 2018. As of August 3, 2022:
https://timothyriecker.com/2018/01/

Roberts, Patrick S., "FEMA and the Prospects for Reputation-Based Autonomy," *Studies in American Political Development*, Vol. 20, No. 1, 2006.

Roberts, Patrick S., *Disasters and the American State: How Politicians, Bureaucrats, and the Public Prepare for the Unexpected*, Cambridge University Press, 2013.

Roberts, Patrick S., "The Lessons of Civil Defense Federalism for the Homeland Security Era," *Journal of Policy History*, Vol. 26, No. 3, 2014.

Robinson, Scott E., and Nicola Mallik, "Varieties of Homeland Security: An Assessment of US State-Level Definitions," *Journal of Homeland Security and Emergency Management*, Vol. 12, No. 1, 2015.

Sandy Recovery Improvement Act of 2013—*See* Public Law 113-2, 2013.

Santayana, George, *The Life of Reason: Introduction and Reason in Common Sense*, Charles Scribner's Sons, 1905.

Schwartz, Heather L., David Grant, Melissa Kay Diliberti, Gerald P. Hunter, and Claude Messan Setodji, *Remote Learning Is Here to Stay: Results from the First American School District Panel Survey*, RAND Corporation, RR-A956-1, 2020. As of November 5, 2022:
https://www.rand.org/pubs/research_reports/RRA956-1.html

Select Bipartisan Committee to Investigate the Preparation for and Response to Hurricane Katrina, U.S. House of Representatives, *A Failure of Initiative: Final Report of the Select Bipartisan Committee to Investigate the Preparation for and Response to Hurricane Katrina*, 109th Cong., 2nd Sess., Report 109-377, February 15, 2006.

Select Committee on Homeland Security, U.S. House of Representatives, *H.R. 5005, The Homeland Security Act of 2002, Day 3*, hearing, 107th Cong., 2nd Sess., July 17, 2002.

Select Committee on Homeland Security, U.S. House of Representatives, *How Is America Safer? A Progress Report on the Department of Homeland Security*, hearing, 108th Cong., 1st Sess., May 20, 2003, and May 22, 2003a.

Select Committee on Homeland Security, U.S. House of Representatives, *Hearing on Response to Terrorism: How Is the Department of Homeland Security Improving Our Capabilities*, 108th Cong., 2nd Sess., June 19, 2003b.

Sharro, Stephen, "How EMI Trains for and Responds to Disasters," *911 Magazine*, March–April 1995.

Sharro, Stephen, "Leadership in a Time of Great Change," Emergency Management Institute, Federal Emergency Management Agency, U.S. Department of Homeland Security, 2021.

Singer, Eric Stephen, *Saving City X: Planners, Citizens and the Culture of Civil Defense in Baltimore, 1950–1964*, doctoral dissertation, American University, 2012.

Smith, Peter L., and Joseph M. Bishop, *Proceedings of the Natural Hazards Management Seminar*, Emergency Management Institute, February 23–27, 1981, c. 1981.

Special Interest Group Working Group on Ethics, Federal Emergency Management Agency, U.S. Department of Homeland Security, "Code of Ethics and Professional Conduct for Emergency Management Professionals," draft under review through December 31, 2021.

Stafford Act, 1988—*See* Public Law 93-288, 1974; Public Law 100-707, 1988; and 42 U.S.C. Chapter 68.

Stampnitzky, Lisa, *Disciplining Terror: How Experts Invented "Terrorism,"* Cambridge University Press, 2013.

Stencel, Mark, "A Nuclear Nightmare in Pennsylvania," *Washington Post*, March 27, 1999.

Stern, Jeffrey, "EMI Anywhere," briefing slides, Federal Emergency Management Agency, U.S. Department of Homeland Security, July 2, 2021.

Stivers, Camilla, "'So Poor and So Black': Hurricane Katrina, Public Administration, and the Issue of Race," *Public Administration Review*, Vol. 67, December 2007.

Stolberg, Alan G., *How Nation-States Craft National Security Strategy Documents*, Strategic Studies Institute, U.S. Army War College, October 2012.

Strope, Jerry, "Scandal Strikes at FEMA," *Journal of Civil Defense*, October 1984.

Subcommittee on Economic Development, Public Buildings, and Emergency Management; Committee on Transportation and Infrastructure; U.S. House of Representatives, *The Federal Emergency Management Agency's Preparedness and Response to All Hazards*, hearing, 110th Cong., 1st Sess., April 26, 2007a.

Subcommittee on Economic Development, Public Buildings, and Emergency Management; Committee on Transportation and Infrastructure; U.S. House of Representatives, *Readiness in the Post-Katrina and Post-9/11 World: An Examination of the New National Response Framework*, hearing, 110th Cong., 1st Sess., September 11, 2007b.

Subcommittee on Emergency Communications, Preparedness, and Response; Committee on Homeland Security; U.S. House of Representatives, *Moving Beyond the First Five Years: Ensuring FEMA's Ability to Respond and Recover in the Wake of a National Catastrophe*, hearing, 110th Cong., 2nd Sess., April 9, 2008.

Subcommittee on Emergency Communications, Preparedness, and Response; Committee on Homeland Security; U.S. House of Representatives, *PKEMRA Implementation: An Examination of FEMA's Preparedness and Response Mission*, hearing, 111th Cong., 1st Sess., March 17, 2009.

Subcommittee on Emergency Preparedness, Science, and Technology; Committee on Homeland Security; U.S. House of Representatives, *The Proposed Fiscal Year 2007 Budget: Enhancing Preparedness for First Responders*, hearing, 109th Cong., 2nd Sess., February 8, 2006.

Subcommittee on Emergency Preparedness, Science, and Technology and Subcommittee on Management, Integration, and Oversight; Committee on Homeland Security, U.S. House of Representatives, *The National Training Program: Is Anti-Terrorism Training for First Responders Efficient and Effective?* 109th Cong., 1st Sess., June 23, 2005.

Subcommittee on International Security, Proliferation, and Federal Services; Committee on Governmental Affairs; U.S. Senate, *FEMA's Role in Managing Bioterrorist Attacks and the Impact of Public Health Concerns on Bioterrorism Preparedness*, hearing, 107th Cong., 1st Sess., July 23, 2001.

Subcommittee on Investigations and Oversight, Committee on Science and Technology, U.S. House of Representatives, *Oversight: Federal Emergency Management Agency*, 98th Cong., 2nd Sess., October 24, 1984.

Subcommittee on Investigations and Oversight, Committee on Science and Technology, U.S. House of Representatives, *Oversight: Federal Emergency Management Agency*, 99th Cong., 1st Sess., March 4, 1985.

Subcommittee on Military Installations and Facilities, Committee on Armed Services, U.S. House of Representatives, *Civil Defense and the Three Mile Island Nuclear Accident: Report of the Military Installations and Facilities Subcommittee of the Committee on Armed Services*, 96th Cong., 1st Sess., December 18, 1979.

Subcommittee on National Security, Veterans Affairs, and International Relations; Committee on Government Reform; U.S. House of Representatives, *Combating Terrorism: Proposed Transfer of the Domestic Preparedness Program*, 106th Cong., 1st Sess., May 26, 1999.

Subcommittee on Technology and Innovation, Committee on Science and Technology, U.S. House of Representatives, *The United States Fire Administration Reauthorization: Addressing the Priorities of the Nation's Fire Service*, hearing, 110th Cong., 1st Sess., October 2, 2007.

Subcommittee on VA-HUD-Independent Agencies; Committee on Appropriations; U.S. Senate, *Departments of Veterans Affairs and Housing and Urban Development and Independent Agencies Appropriations for Fiscal Year 1998*, hearings, 105th Cong., 1st Sess., 1998.

Swindle, John L., Henry D. Smith, and David M. McCormack, *Report of the National Academy for Fire Prevention and Control Site Selection Board*, National Fire Prevention and Control Administration, U.S. Department of Commerce, 1976.

Tennent, James, "To Keep Students Safe, Oklahoma Is Using Bulletproof Storm Shelters at Elementary and Middle Schools," *Newsweek*, February 28, 2018.

Thornton, Patricia H., and William Ocasio, "Institutional Logics and the Historical Contingency of Power in Organizations: Executive Succession in the Higher Education Publishing Industry, 1958–1990," *American Journal of Sociology*, Vol. 105, No. 3, November 1999.

Thornton, Patricia H., William Ocasio, and Michael Lounsbury, *The Institutional Logics Perspective: A New Approach to Culture, Structure, and Process*, Oxford University Press, 2012.

Tierney, Kathleen J., "Testimony on Needed Emergency Management Reforms," *Journal of Homeland Security and Emergency Management*, Vol. 4, No. 3, 2007.

Tolbert, Eric, director, Response Division, Federal Emergency Management Agency, U.S. Department of Homeland Security, statement for a hearing titled *Terror Attacks: Are We Prepared?* before the Committee on Health, Education, Labor, and Pensions, U.S. Senate, 108th Cong., 2nd Sess., July 22, 2004.

Truman, Harry S., "Executive Order 10186: Establishing the Federal Civil Defense Administration in the Office for Emergency Management of the Executive Office of the President," *Federal Register*, December 1, 1950.

U.S. Bureau of Labor Statistics, U.S. Department of Labor, "Emergency Management Directors: Summary," *Occupational Outlook Handbook*, last modified April 18, 2022.

U.S. Code, Title 6, Domestic Security; Chapter 1, Homeland Security Organization; Subchapter III, Science and Technology in Support of Homeland Security; Section 185, Federally Funded Research and Development Centers.

U.S. Code, Title 42, The Public Health and Welfare; Chapter 68, Disaster Relief.

U.S. Department of Homeland Security, *Quadrennial Homeland Security Review Report: A Strategic Framework for a Secure Homeland*, February 2010.

U.S. Department of Homeland Security, *U.S. Department of Homeland Security Annual Performance Report: Fiscal Years 2012–2014*, April 1, 2013.

U.S. Department of Homeland Security, *The 2014 Quadrennial Homeland Security Review*, June 18, 2014.

U.S. Department of Homeland Security, fiscal year 2015 budget justification, c. 2015a.

U.S. Department of Homeland Security, *National Preparedness Goal*, 2nd ed., September 2015b.

U.S. Department of Homeland Security, *Congressional Budget Justification: FY 2016*, c. 2016.

U.S. Department of Homeland Security, *Congressional Budget Justification: FY 2017—Volume III, U.S. Secret Service, National Protection and Programs Directorate, Federal Emergency Management Agency, U.S. Citizenship and Immigration Services*, c. 2017.

U.S. Department of Homeland Security, "Operation Allies Welcome Announces Departure of All Afghan Nationals from U.S. Military Bases," press release, February 19, 2022.

USFA—*See* U.S. Fire Administration.

U.S. Fire Administration, *U.S. Fire Administration 25th Anniversary: Challenging Fire in America for 25 Years*, 1999.

U.S. Government Accountability Office, *Catastrophic Disasters: Enhanced Leadership, Capabilities, and Accountability Controls Will Improve Effectiveness of the Nation's Preparedness, Response, and Recovery System*, GAO 06-618, September 6, 2006.

U.S. Government Accountability Office, *FEMA Disaster Workforce: Actions Needed to Address Deployment and Staff Development Challenges*, GAO-20-360, May 4, 2020.

U.S. House of Representatives, "Conference Report on H.R. 2684, Departments of Veterans Affairs and Housing and Urban Development, and Independent Agencies Appropriations Act, 2000," *Congressional Record*, Vol. 145, No. 138, October 13, 1999.

U.S. Senate, "Amendments Proposed and Submitted," *Congressional Record*, Vol. 164, No. 96, June 11, 2018.

Vanguard Senior Executive Leadership Program, "After Action Report," June 27, 2022.

Vergano, Dan, "The US Government Is Updating Its Nuclear Disaster Plans and They Are Truly Terrifying," *Buzzfeed News*, August 24, 2018.

Vogel, Pete, and Shane Gibbon, *EMI 60th Anniversary*, DVD, Emergency Management Institute, Federal Emergency Management Agency, U.S. Department of Homeland Security, 2011.

Walker, Mike, deputy director, Federal Emergency Management Agency, statement for the record before the Subcommittee on Government Management, Information, and Technology; Committee on Government Reform; U.S. House of Representatives hearing titled "Year 2000 Emergency Management," 106th Cong., 1st Sess., March 22, 1999.

Wamsley, Gary L., *Coping with Catastrophe: Building an Emergency Management System to Meet People's Needs in Natural and Manmade Disasters*, National Academy of Public Administration, 1993.

Waugh, William L., Jr., "The 'All-Hazards' Approach Must Be Continued," *Journal of Emergency Management*, Vol. 2, No. 1, 2004.

Waugh, William L., Jr., "Shelter from the Storm: Repairing the National Emergency Management System After Hurricane Katrina," *Annals of the American Academy of Political and Social Science*, Vol. 604, No. 1, March 2006.

Waugh, William L., Jr., "Local Emergency Management in the Post-9/11 World," in William L. Waugh, Jr., and Kathleen J. Tierney, eds., *Emergency Management: Principles and Practice for Local Government*, 2nd ed., International City Management Association Press, 2007.

Waugh, William L., Jr., and Kay C. Goss, "The History of Higher Education in Emergency Management: The Emergency Management Institute, the National Science Foundation, and the William Averette Anderson Fund," *Journal of Emergency Management (Weston, Mass.)*, Vol. 17, No. 1, January–February 2019.

Weaver, John, Lindsey C. Harkabus, Jeffry Braun, Steven Miller, Rob Cox, John Griffith, and Rebecca J. Mazur, "An Overview of a Demographic Study of United States Emergency Managers," *Bulletin of the American Meteorological Society*, Vol. 95, No. 2, 2014.

White House, "Executive Summary," webpage, April 2002. As of July 7, 2022:
https://georgewbush-whitehouse.archives.gov/news/releases/2002/04/summary.html

White House, "President Biden Announces Team to Lead Monkeypox Response," news release, August 2, 2022.

Wilensky, Harold L., "The Professionalization of Everyone?" *American Journal of Sociology*, Vol. 70, No. 2, September 1964.

William Averette Anderson Fund, "Mission," webpage, undated. As of November 5, 2022:
https://billandersonfund.org/purpose

Wilson, Jennifer, "Professionalization and Gender in Local Emergency Management," *International Journal of Mass Emergencies and Disasters*, Vol. 17, No. 1, March 1999.

Witt, James Lee, and James Morgan, *Stronger in the Broken Places: Nine Lessons for Turning Crisis into Triumph*, Times Books, 2002.

"Witt Reinvents FEMA," *Natural Hazards Observer*, No. 2, November 1993.

Xu, H. Daniel, and Rashmita Basu, "How the United States Flunked the COVID-19 Test: Some Observations and Several Lessons," *American Review of Public Administration*, Vol. 50, No. 6–7, August–October 2020.

Milton Keynes UK
Ingram Content Group UK Ltd.
UKHW052311031123
431725UK00007B/24